Günter Grass was born in Danzig in 1927. He is Germany's most celebrated contemporary writer. Though best known as a novelist – author of The Danzig Trilogy (*The Tin Drum*, *Cat and Mouse* and *Dog Years*) and *The Flounder* – he is also poet, playwright, sculptor, graphic artist, essayist and political spokesman.

Günter Grass

CAT
and MOUSE

Translated by Ralph Manheim

published by Pan Books

Katz und Maus first published in Germany 1961
this translation first published in Great Britain
by Martin Secker & Warburg Ltd 1963
This Picador edition published 1989 by
Pan Books Ltd, Cavaye Place, London SW10 9PG
9 8 7 6 5 4 3 2 1
© Hermann Lucherhand Verlag GmbH 1961
Translation © Harcourt, Brace & World, Inc. and
Martin Secker & Warburg Ltd 1963
All rights reserved
ISBN 0 330 30556 5
Printed and bound in Great Britain by
Cox & Wyman Ltd, Reading

Chapter One

... And one day, after Mahlke had learned to swim, we were lying in the grass, in the Schlagball field. I ought to have gone to the dentist, but they wouldn't let me because I was hard to replace on the team. My tooth was howling. A cat sauntered diagonally across the field and no one threw anything at it. A few of the boys were chewing or plucking at blades of grass. The cat belonged to the caretaker and was black. Hotten Sonntag rubbed his bat with a woollen stocking. My tooth marked time. The tournament had been going on for two hours. We had lost hands down and were waiting for the return game. It was a young cat, but no kitten. In the stadium, handball goals were being made thick and fast on both sides. My tooth kept saying one word, over and over again. On the cinder track the sprinters were practising starts or limbering up. The cat meandered about. A tri-motored plane crept across the sky, slow and loud, but couldn't drown out my tooth. Through the grass stalks the caretaker's black cat showed a white bib. Mahlke was asleep. The wind was from the east, and the crematorium between the United Cemeteries and the Engineering School was operating. Mr Mallenbrandt, the gym teacher, blew his whistle: Change sides. The cat practised. Mahlke was asleep or seemed to be. I was next to him with my toothache. Still practising, the cat came closer. Mahlke's Adam's apple attracted attention because it was large, always in motion, and threw a shadow. Between me and Mahlke the caretaker's black cat tensed for a leap. We formed a triangle. My tooth was silent and stopped marking time: for Mahlke's Adam's apple had become the cat's mouse. It was so young a cat, and Mahlke's whatsis was so active – in any case the cat leapt at Mahlke's throat; or one of us caught the cat and held it up to Mahlke's neck; or I, with or without my toothache, seized the cat and showed it Mahlke's mouse: and Joachim Mahlke let out a yell, but suffered only slight scratches.

And now it is up to me, who called your mouse to the attention of this cat and all cats, to write. Even if we were both invented, I should have to write. Over and over again the fellow who invented us because it's his business to invent people obliges me to take your Adam's apple in my hand and carry it to the spot that saw it win or lose. And so, to begin with, I make the mouse bob up and down above the screwdriver, I fling a multitude of replete sea-gulls into the fitful northeast wind, high over Mahlke's head, call the weather summery and persistently fair, assume that the wreck was a former mine sweeper of the *Czaika* class, and give the Baltic the colour of thick-glass seltzer bottles. Now that the scene of action has been identified as a point southeast of the Neufahrwasser harbour buoy, I make Mahlke's skin, from which water is still running in rivulets, take on a texture somewhere between fine and coarse-grained. It was not fear, however, that roughened Mahlke's skin, but the shivers customary after long immersion in the sea that seized hold of Mahlke and took the smoothness from his skin.

And yet none of us, as we huddled lean and long armed between our upthrust knees on the remains of the bridge, had asked Mahlke to dive down again into the fo'c'sle of the sunken mine sweeper and the adjoining engine room amidships, and work something loose with his screwdriver, a screw, a little wheel, or something really special: a brass plate inscribed with the directions in Polish and English for operating some machine. We were sitting on

6

the superstructure, or as much of it as remained above the water, of a former Polish mine sweeper of the *Czaika* class, built in Gdynia and launched in Modlin, which had been sunk the year before southeast of the harbour buoy, well outside the channel so that it did not interfere with shipping.

Since then gull droppings had dried on the rust. In all kinds of weather the gulls flew sleek and smooth, with eyes like glass beads on the sides of their heads, grazing the remains of the pilot house, then wildly up again, according to some indecipherable plan, squirting their slimy droppings in full flight – and they never fell into the soft sea but always on the rusty superstructure. Hard, dense, calcareous, the droppings clung fast, side by side in innumerable spots, or heaped up in mounds. And always when we sat on the barge, fingernails and toenails tried to chip off the droppings. That's why our nails cracked and not because we bit our fingernails – except for Schilling who was always chewing at them and had nails like rivets. Only Mahlke had long nails, though they were yellow from all his diving, and he kept them long by neither biting them nor scratching at the gull droppings. And he was the only one who never ate the chips we broke loose – the rest of us, because it was there, chewed the stony, shell-like mess into a foaming slime, which we spat overboard. The stuff tasted like nothing at all or like plaster or like fish meal or like everything imaginable: happiness, girls, God in His heaven. 'Do you realize,' said Winter, who sang very nicely, 'that tenors eat gull droppings every day?' Often the gulls caught our calcareous spittle in full flight, apparently suspecting nothing.

When shortly after the outbreak of the war Joachim Mahlke turned fourteen, he could neither swim nor ride a bicycle; there was nothing striking about his appearance and he lacked the Adam's apple which was later to lure the cat. He had been excused from gymnastics and swimming, because he had presented certificates showing him to be sickly. Even before he learned to ride a bicycle – a ludicrous figure with his deep red, protuberant ears and his knees thrust sideways as he pedalled – he reported for swimming in the winter season, at the Niederstadt pool, but at first he was admitted only to the 'dry swimming' class for eight to ten year-olds. Nor did he make much progress the following summer. The swimming teacher at Brösen Beach, a typical swimming teacher with a torso like a life-buoy and thin hairless legs, had to put Mahlke through his paces in the sand and then hold him up by a life-line. But after we had swum away from him several afternoons in a row and come back telling fantastic stories about the sunken mine sweeper, he was mightily inspired and in less than two weeks he was swimming.

Earnestly and conscientiously he swam back and forth between the pier, the big diving tower, and the bathing beach, and he had no doubt achieved a certain endurance by the time he began to practise diving off the little break-water outside the pier, first bringing up some common Baltic mussels, then diving for a beer bottle filled with sand, which he threw out pretty far. My guess is that Mahlke soon succeeded in recovering the bottle quite regularly, for when he began to dive with us on the mine sweeper, he was no longer a beginner.

He pleaded with us to let him come along. Six or seven of us were getting ready for our daily swim, elaborately moistening our skins in the shallow water of the family pool, as a precaution against sudden chill. And there was Mahlke on the plank walk: 'Please take me with you. I'm sure I can do it.'

A screwdriver hung round his neck, distracting attention from his Adam's apple.

'OK!' And Mahlke came along. Between the first and second sandbank he passed us, and we didn't bother

8

to catch up with him. 'Let him knock himself out.'

When Mahlke swam breaststroke, the screwdriver bobbed visibly up and down between his shoulder blades, for it had a wooden handle. When he swam on his back, the wooden handle danced about on his chest, but never entirely covered the horrid piece of cartilage between chin and collarbone, which cut through the water like a dorsal fin, leaving a wake behind it.

And then Mahlke showed us. He dived several times in quick succession with his screwdriver and brought up whatever he was able to unscrew: lids, pieces of sheathing, a part of the generator; he found a rope, and with the help of the broken-down winch hoisted up a genuine fire extinguisher from the fo'c'sle. The thing – made in Germany, I might add – still worked; Mahlke proved it, squirting streams of foam to show us how you extinguish with foam, extinguishing the glass-green sea – from the very first day he was an ace.

The flakes still lay in islands and long streaks on the flat even swell, attracting a few gulls which were soon repelled, settled and like a big mess of whipped cream turned sour, drifted off toward the beach. Then Mahlke called it a day and sat down in the shadow of the pilot house; and even before the stray tatters of foam on the bridge had time to lose their stiffness and start trembling in the breeze, his skin had taken on that shrivelled, coarse-grained look.

Mahlke shivered and his Adam's apple jogged up and down; his screwdriver did dance steps over his quaking collarbones. His back, white in spots, burned lobster-red from the shoulders down, which was forever peeling with fresh sunburn on both sides of his prominent spinal column, was also covered with gooseflesh and shaken with fitful shudders. His yellowish lips, blue at the edges, bared his chattering teeth. But he tried to bring his body – and his teeth – under control by clasping his knees, which he

9

had bruised on the barnacle-covered bulkheads, with his big waterlogged hands.

Hotten Sonntag – or was it I? – rubbed Mahlke down. 'Lord, man, don't go catching something. We've still got to get back.' The screwdriver began to calm down.

The way out took us twenty-five minutes from the breakwater, thirty-five from the beach. We needed a good threequarters of an hour to get back. No matter how exhausted he was, he was always standing on the breakwater a good minute ahead of us. He never lost the lead he had taken the first day. Before we reached the barge – as we called the mine sweeper – Mahlke had already been under once, and as soon as we reached out our washer-woman's hands, all of us pretty much at once, for the rust and gull droppings of the bridge or the jutting gun mounts, he silently exhibited a hinge or something or other that had come off easily, and already he was shivering, though after the second or third time he covered himself with a thick, extravagant coat of Nivea cream; for Mahlke had plenty of pocket money.

Mahlke was an only child.

Mahlke was half an orphan.

Mahlke's father was dead.

Winter and summer Mahlke wore old-fashioned boots which he must have inherited from his father.

He carried the screwdriver round his neck on a shoelace for black boots.

It occurs to me only now that, in addition to the screwdriver, Mahlke, for certain reasons, wore something else round his neck; but the screwdriver was more conspicuous.

He wore a little silver chain, from which hung something silver and Catholic: the Blessed Virgin; most likely he had always worn it, but we had never noticed; he certainly had it on ever since the day when he started to

10

swim in harness and to make figures in the sand while practising his kick.

Never, not even in gym class, did Mahlke remove the medal from his neck; for no sooner had he taken up dry swimming and swimming in harness in the winter swimming pool at Niederstadt than he turned up in our gymnasium, and never again did he produce any doctor's certificates. Either the silver Virgin disappeared under his white gym shirt or lay just over the red stripe that ran around it at chest level.

Even the parallel bars held no horrors for Mahlke. Only three or four of the best members of the first squad were equal to the horse exercises, but Mahlke was right with them, leaping from the springboard, sailing over the long leather horse, and landing on the mat with Virgin awry, sending up clouds of dust. When he did knee-springs on the horizontal bar – his form was miserable, but later, he succeeded in doing two more than Hotten Sonntag, our gymnastics champion – well, when Mahlke ground out his thirty-seven knee-springs, the medal tugged out of his gym shirt, and hurtled thirty-seven times round the squeaking horizontal bar, always in advance of his medium-brown hair. But it never came free from his neck, for the wildly agitated chain was held in place not only by his jutting Adam's apple, but also by his protuberant occiput with its thick growth of hair.

The screwdriver lay over the medal, and in places the shoelace covered the chain. However, the screwdriver did not outshine the medal, especially as the object with the wooden handle was not allowed in the gymnasium. Our gym teacher, a Mr Mallenbrandt who was also assistant principal and was well known in sports circles because he had written a rule book to end all rule books for the game of Schlagball, forbade Mahlke to wear the screwdriver round his neck in gym class. Mallenbrandt never found any fault with the medal on Mahlke's neck, because in addition to physical culture and geography, he taught religion, and up to the second year of the war guided the remnants of a Catholic workers' gymnastic society over and under the horizontal and parallel bars.

And so the screwdriver had to wait in the dressing room, over his shirt on the hook, while the slightly worn, silver Virgin was privileged to hang from Mahlke's neck and succour him amid gymnastic perils.

A common screwdriver it was, cheap and sturdy. Often Mahlke, in order to detach a small plaque no larger than the name plate beside an apartment door, had to dive five or six times, especially when the plate was affixed to metal and the screws were rusted. On the other hand, he sometimes managed, after only two dives, to bring up larger plaques with long texts inscribed on them by using his screwdriver as a jemmy and prying screws and all from the waterlogged wooden sheathing. He was no great collector; he gave many of his plaques to Winter and Jürgen Kupka, who fanatically collected everything removable, including street markers and the signs in public toilets; for himself he took only the few items that particularly struck his fancy.

Mahlke didn't make things easy for himself; while we dozed on the barge, he worked under water. We scratched at the gull droppings and turned brown as cigars; those of us who had blond hair were transformed into tow-heads. Mahlke at most took on fresh lobster tones. While we followed the ships north of the beacon, he looked unswervingly downward: reddened, slightly inflamed lids with sparse lashes, I think; light-blue eyes which filled with curiosity only under water. Sometimes Mahlke came up without any plaques or other spoils, but with a broken or hopelessly bent screwdriver. That too he would exhibit and always got an effect. The gesture with which he tossed it over his shoulder into the water, exasperating the gulls, was commanded neither by resigned disappointment nor aimless rage. Never did Mahlke throw away a broken tool with indifference, real or affected. Even this act of tossing away signified: I'll soon have something more to show you.

. . . and once – a hospital ship with two smokestacks had put into port, and after a brief discussion we had identified it as the *Kaiser* of the East Prussian Maritime Service – Joachim Mahlke went down into the fo'c'sle without a screwdriver, and holding his nose with two fingers, vanished in the open, slate-green, slightly submerged forward hatchway. He went in head first – his hair was plastered flat and parted from swimming and diving; he pulled in his back and hips, kicked once at the empty air, but then, bracing both feet against the edge of the hatch, pushed down into the dusky cool aquarium, floodlit through open portholes: nervous sticklebacks, an immobile school of lampreys, swaying hammocks, still firmly attached at the ends, overgrown with seaweed, a playhouse for baby herring. Rarely a stray cod. Only rumours of eels. We never once saw a flounder.

We clasped our slightly trembling knees, chewed gull droppings into a sludge; half weary, half fascinated, we counted a formation of Navy cutters, followed the stacks of the hospital ship, whence smoke was still rising vertically, exchanged sidelong glances. He stayed down a long while – gulls circled, the swell gurgled over the bow, broke against the forward gun mountings – the gun itself had been removed. A splashing as the water flowed back between the ventilators behind the bridge, licking always at the same rivets; lime under fingernails; itching on dry skin, shimmering light, chugging of motors in the wind, private parts half-stiff, seventeen poplars between Brösen and Glettkau – and then he came shooting upward: bluish-red around the chin, yellowish over the cheekbones. His hair parted exactly in the middle, he rose like a

13

fountain from the hatch, staggered over the bow through water up to his knees, reached for the jutting gun mounts, and fell watery-goggle-eyed to his knees; we had to pull him up on the bridge. But before the water had stopped flowing from his nose and the corner of his mouth, he showed us his find, a steel screwdriver in one piece. Made in England. Stamped on the metal: Sheffield. No scars, no rust, still coated with grease. The water formed into beads and rolled off.

Every day for over a year Mahlke wore this heavy, to all intents and purposes unbreakable screwdriver on a shoelace, even after we had stopped or almost stopped swimming out to the barge. Though he was a good Catholic, it became a kind of cult with him. Before gym class, for instance, he would give the thing to Mr Mallenbrandt for safekeeping, he was dreadfully afraid it might be stolen, and even took it with him to St Mary's Chapel; for not only on Sunday, but also on week days, he went to early Mass on Marineweg, not far from the Neuschottland cooperative housing development.

He and his English screwdriver didn't have far to go – out of Osterzeile and down Bärenweg. Quantities of two-storey houses, villas with gable roofs, porticos, and espaliered fruit trees. Then two rows of housing developments, plain drab walls ornamented only with water spots. To the right the streetcar line turned off and with it the overhead wires, mostly against a partly cloudy sky. To the left, the sandy, sorry looking kitchen gardens of the railway workers: bowers and rabbit hutches built with the black and red boards of abandoned freight cars. Behind the gardens the signals of the railway leading to the Free Port. Silos, movable and stationary cranes. The strange full-coloured superstructures of the freighters. The two grey battleships with their old-fashioned turrets were still there, the swimming dock, the Germania bread factory;

and silvery sleek, at medium height, a few captive balloons, lurching and bobbing. In the right background, the Gudrun School (the Helen-Lange School of former years) blocking out the iron hodge-podge of the Schichau Dockyards as far as the big hammer crane. To this side of it, covered, well-tended athletic fields, freshly painted goalposts, foul lines marked in lime on the short grass: next Sunday Blue-and-Yellow versus Schellmühl 98 – no grandstand, but a modern, tall-windowed gymnasium painted in light ochre. The fresh red roof of this edifice, oddly enough, was topped with a tarred wooden cross; for St Mary's Chapel had formerly been a gymnasium belonging to the Neuschottland Sports Club. It had been found necessary to transform it into an emergency church, because the Church of the Sacred Heart was too far away; for years the people of Neuschottland, Schellmühl, and the housing development between Osterzeile and Westerzeile, mostly shipyard, railway, or post-office workers, had sent petitions to the bishop in Oliva until, still during the Free State period, this gymnasium had been purchased, remodelled, and consecrated.

Despite the tortuous and colourful pictures and ornaments, some privately donated but for the most part deriving from the cellars and storerooms of just about every church in the diocese, there was no denying or concealing the gymnasium quality of this church – no amount of incense or wax candles could drown out the aroma of the chalk, leather, and sweat of former years and former handball matches. And the chapel never lost a certain air of Protestant parsimony, the fanatical sobriety of a meeting house.

In the neo-Gothic Church of the Sacred Heart, built of bricks at the end of the nineteenth century, not far from the suburban railway station, Joachim Mahlke's steel screwdriver would have seemed strange, ugly and sacrilegious. In St Mary's Chapel, on the other hand, he might

15

perfectly well have worn it openly: the little chapel with its well-kept linoleum floor, its rectangular frosted glass window-panes starting just under the ceiling, the neat iron fixtures which had formerly served to hold the horizontal bar firmly in place, the planking in the coarse-grained concrete ceiling, and beneath it the iron (though whitewashed) cross-beams to which the rings, the trapeze, and half a dozen climbing ropes had formerly been affixed, was so modern, so coldly functional a chapel, despite the painted and gilded plaster which bestowed blessing and consecration on all sides, that the steel screwdriver which Mahlke, in prayer and then in communion, felt it necessary to have dangling from his neck, would never have attracted the attention either of the few devotees of early Mass, or of Father Gusewski and his sleepy altar boy – who often enough was myself.

No, there I'm going too far. It would certainly not have escaped me. As often as I served at the altar, even during the gradual prayers, I did my best, for various reasons, to keep an eye on you. And you played safe; you kept your treasure under your shirt, and that was why your shirt had those grease spots vaguely indicating the shape of the screwdriver. Seen from the altar, he knelt in the second pew of the left hand row, aiming his prayer with open eyes – light grey they were, I think, and usually inflamed from all his swimming and diving – in the direction of the Virgin.

. . . and once – I don't remember which summer it was – was it during the first summer vacation on the barge shortly after the row in France, or was it the following summer? – one hot and misty day, enormous crowd on the family beach, sagging pennants, over-ripe flesh, big rush at the refreshments stands, on burning feet over the fibre runners, past locked cabins full of tittering, through a turbulent mob of children engaged in slobbering,

16

tumbling, and cutting their feet; and in the midst of this spawn which would now be twenty-three years old, beneath the solicitous eyes of the grown-ups, a little brat, who must have been about three, pounded monotonously on a child's tin drum, turning the afternoon into an infernal smithy – whereupon we took to the water and swam out to our barge; from the beach, in the lifeguard's binoculars for instance, we were six diminishing heads in motion; one head in advance of the rest and first to reach the goal.

We threw ourselves on burning though wind-cooled rust and gull droppings and lay motionless. Mahlke had already been under twice. He came up with something in his left hand. He had searched the crew's quarters, in and under the half-rotted hammocks, some tossing limply, others still lashed fast, amid swarms of iridescent stickle-backs, through forests of seaweed where lampreys darted in and out, and in a matted mound, once the sea kit of Seaman Duszynski or Liszinski, he had found a bronze medallion the size of a hand, bearing on one side, below a small embossed Polish eagle, the name of the owner and the date on which it had been conferred, and on the other a relief of a mustachio'd general. After a certain amount of rubbing with sand and powdered gull droppings the circular inscription told us that Mahlke had brought to light the portrait of Marshal Pilsudski.

For two weeks Mahlke concentrated on medallions; he also found a kind of tin plate commemorating a regatta in the Gdynia roadstead and amidships, between fo'c'sle and engine room, in the cramped, almost inaccessible officers' mess, a silver medal the size of a mark piece, with a silver ring to pass a chain through; the reverse was flat, worn and anonymous, but the face, amid a profusion of ornament, bore the Virgin and Child in sharp relief.

A raised inscription identified her as the famous

Matka Boska Czestochowska; and when Mahlke on the bridge saw what he had found, we offered him sand, but he did not polish his metal; he preferred the black patina.

The rest of us wanted to see shining silver. But before we had finished arguing, he had knelt down on his knobby knees in the shadow of the pilot house, shifting his treasure about until it was at the right angle for his gaze, lowered in devotion, to fall directly upon it. We laughed as, bluish and shivering, he crossed himself with his waterlogged fingertips, attempted to move his lips in prayer, and produced a bit of Latin between chattering teeth. I still think it was even then something from his favourite sequence, which normally was spoken only on the Friday before Palm Sunday: '*Virgo virginum praeclara. Mihi iam non sis amara . ...*'

Later, after Dr Klohse, our principal, had forbidden Mahlke to wear this Polish article openly on his neck during classes – Klohse was a high party officer, though he seldom wore his uniform at school – Joachim Mahlke contented himself with wearing his usual little amulet and the steel screwdriver beneath the Adam's apple which a cat had taken for a mouse.

He hung the blackened silver Virgin between Pilsudski's bronze profile and the postcard size photo of Commodore Bonte, the hero of Narvik.

Chapter Two

Was all this praying and worshipping in jest? Your house was in Westerzeile. You had a strange sense of humour, if any. No, your house was on Osterzeile. All the streets in the housing development looked alike. And yet you had only to eat a sandwich and we would laugh, each infecting the other. Every time we had to laugh at

18

you, it came as a surprise to us. But when Dr Brunies, one of our teachers, asked the boys of our class what profession they were planning to take and you – you already knew how to swim – said: 'I'm going to be a clown and make people laugh,' no one laughed in the classroom – and I myself was frightened. For while Mahlke firmly and candidly stated his intention of becoming a clown in a circus or somewhere else, he made so solemn a face that it was really to be feared that he would one day make people laugh themselves sick, if only by publicly praying to the Virgin between the lion tamer and the trapeze act; but that prayer of yours on the barge must have been in earnest – or wasn't it?

He lived on Osterzeile and not on Westerzeile. The one-family house stood beside, between, and opposite similar one-family houses which could be distinguished perhaps by different patterns or folds in the curtains, but hardly by the vegetation of the little gardens out in front. And each garden had its little bird house on a pole and its glazed garden ornaments: frogs, mushrooms, or dwarfs. In front of Mahlke's house sat a ceramic frog. But in front of the next house and the next, there were also green ceramic frogs.

In short, it was number twenty-four, and when you approached from Wolfsweg, Mahlke lived in the fourth house on the left side of the street. Like Westerzeile which ran parallel to it, Osterzeile was perpendicular to Bärenweg, which ran parallel to Wolfsweg. When you went down Westerzeile from the Wolfsweg and looked leftward and westward over the red tiled roofs, you saw the west side and front of a tower with a tarnished bulbi-form steeple. If you went down Osterzeile in the same direction, you saw over the rooftops the east side and front of the same belfry; for Christ Church lay on the far side of Bärenweg, exactly halfway between Osterzeile

19

and Westerzeile, and with its four dials beneath the green, bulbiform roof, provided the whole neighbourhood, from Max-Halbe-Platz to the Catholic and clockless St Mary's Chapel, from Magdeburger Strasse to Posadowski-weg near Schellmühl with the time of day, enabling Protestant as well as Catholic factory workers and office workers, salesgirls and schoolboys to reach their schools or places of work with interdenominational punctuality.

From his window Mahlke could see the dial of the east face of the tower. He had his room in the attic; the walls were slightly on a slant, and the rain and hail beat down directly over his head: an attic room full of the usual juvenile bric-à-brac, from the butterfly collection to the postcard photos of movie stars, lavishly decorated fighter pilots and Panzer generals; but in the midst of all this, an unframed colour print of the Sistine Madonna with the two chubby cheeked angels at the lower edge, the Pilsudski medal, already mentioned, and the consecrated amulet from Czestochowa beside a photograph of the commander of the Narvik destroyers.

The very first time I went to see him, I noticed the stuffed snowy owl. I lived quite near, on Westerzeile; but I'm not going to speak of myself, my story is about Mahlke, or Mahlke and me, but always with the emphasis on Mahlke, for his hair was parted in the middle, he wore boots, he always had something or other dangling from his neck to distract the eternal cat from the eternal mouse, he knelt at the altar of Our Lady, he was the diver with the fresh sunburn; though he was always tied up in knots and his form was bad, he always had a bit of a lead on the rest of us, and no sooner had he learned to swim than he made up his mind that some day, after finishing school and all that, he would be a clown in the circus and make people laugh.

The snowy owl had Mahlke's solemn parting in the

20

middleand the same suffering, meekly resolute look, as of a redeemer plagued by inner toothache. It was well prepared, only discreetly retouched, and held a birch branch in its claws. The owl had been left him by his father.

I did my best to ignore the snowy owl, the colour print of the Madonna, and the silver piece from Czestochowa; for me the centre of the room was the gramophone which Mahlke had painstakingly raised from the barge. He had found no records; they must have dissolved. It was a relatively modern contrivance with a crank and a player arm. He had found it in the same officers' mess that had already yielded up his silver medal and several other items. The cabin was amidships, hence inaccessible to the rest of us, even Hotten Sonntag. For we only went as far as the fo'c'sle and never ventured through the dark bulkhead, which even the fishes seldom visited, into the engine room and the cramped adjoining cabins.

Shortly before the end of our first summer vacation on the barge, Mahlke brought up the gramophone – German-made it was, like the fire extinguisher – after perhaps a dozen dives. Inch by inch he had moved it forward to the foot of the hatch and finally hoisted it up to us on the bridge with the help of the same rope that had served for the fire extinguisher.

We had to improvise a raft of driftwood and cork to haul the thing ashore; the crank was frozen with rust. We took turns in towing the raft, all of us except Mahlke.

A week later the gramophone was in his room, repaired, oiled, the metal part freshly plated. The turntable was covered with fresh felt. After winding it in my presence, he set the rich-green turntable revolving empty. Mahlke stood behind it with folded arms, beside the snowy owl on its birch branch. His mouse was quiet. I stood with my back to the Sistine colour print, gazing either at the empty, slightly wobbling turntable, or out of the mansard window, over the raw-red roof tiles, at Christ Church, one dial on the front, another on the east side of the bulbiform tower. Before the clock struck six, the gramophone droned to a stop. Mahlke wound the thing up again, demanding that I give his new rite my unflagging attention: I listened to the assortment of soft and medium sounds characteristic of an antique gramophone left to its own devices. Mahlke had as yet no records.

There were books on a long sagging shelf. He read a good deal, including religious works. In addition to the cacti on the window-sill, to models of a torpedo boat of the *Wolff* class and the dispatch boat *Cricket*, I must also mention a glass of water which always stood on the washstand beside the bowl; the water was cloudy and there was an inch-thick layer of sugar at the bottom. In this glass Mahlke each morning, with sugar and care, stirred up the milky solution designed to hold his thin, limp hair in place; he never removed the sediment of the previous day. Once he offered me the preparation and I combed the sugar water into my hair: it must be admitted that thanks to his fixative, my hairdo preserved a vitreous rigidity until evening: my scalp itched, my hands were sticky, like Mahlke's hands, from passing them over my hair to see how it was doing – but maybe the stickiness of my hands is only an idea that came to me later, maybe they were not sticky at all.

Below him, in three rooms of which only two were used, lived his mother and her elder sister. Both of them quiet as mice when he was there, always worried and proud of the boy, for to judge by his report cards Mahlke was a good student, though not at the head of the class. He was – and this detracted slightly from the merit of his performance – a year older than the rest of us, because his mother and aunt had sent the frail, or as they put it sickly, lad to secondary school a year later than usual.

But he was no swot, he studied with moderation, let everyone copy from him, never told tales, showed no particular zeal except in gym class, and had a conspicuous horror of the nasty practical jokes customary in Third Form. He interfered, for instance, when Hotten Sonntag, having found a condom in Staffenspark, brought it to class mounted on a branch, and stretched it over our classroom door knob. The intended victim was Dr Treuge, a doddering half-blind pedant, who ought to have been pensioned years before. A voice called from the corridor: 'He's coming,' whereupon Mahlke arose, strode without haste to the door, and removed the loathsome object with a sandwich paper.

No one said a word. Once more he had shown us; and today I can say that in everything he did or did not do – in not being a swot, in studying with moderation, in allowing all and sundry to copy from him, in showing no particular zeal except in gym class, in shunning nasty practical jokes, he was always that very special, individual Mahlke, always, with or without effort, gathering applause. After all he was planning to go into the circus later or maybe on the stage; to remove loathsome objects from doorknobs was to practise his clowning; he received murmurs of approval and was almost a clown when he did his knee swings on the horizontal bar, whirling his silver Virgin through the fetid vapours of the gymnasium. But Mahlke piled up the most applause in summer vacation on the sunken barge, although it would scarcely have occurred to us to consider his frantic diving as a circus act. And we never laughed when Mahlke, time and time again, climbed blue and shivering on to the barge, bringing up something or other in order to show us what he had brought up. At most we said with thoughtful admiration: 'I say, that's super. I wish I had your nerves. You're a cool 'un all right. How'd you ever get that loose?'

Applause did him good and quietened the jumping mouse on his throat; applause also embarrassed him and started the selfsame mouse up again. Usually he made a disparaging gesture, which brought him new applause. He wasn't one for brag; never once did he say: 'You try it.' Or: 'I dare one of you to try.' Or: 'Remember the day before yesterday, the way I went down four times, one after the other, the way I went in amidships as far as the galley and brought up that wonderful tin of food. None of you ever did that. I bet it came from France, there were frogs' legs in it, tasted something like veal, but you were a bunch of yellowbellies, you wouldn't even try it after I'd eaten half the tin. And damned if I didn't get a second tin, and a can opener too, but the second was stinking, rotten corned beef.'

No, Mahlke never spoke like that. He did extra-ordinary things. One day, for instance, he crawled into the barge's one-time galley, and brought up several tins of food, which according to the inscriptions stamped in the metal were of English or French origin; he even located an almost serviceable tin opener. Without a word he ripped the tins before our eyes, devoured the alleged frogs' legs, his Adam's apple doing push-ups as he chewed – I forgot to say that Mahlke was by nature an eater – and when the tin was half empty, he held it out to us, invitingly but not overbearingly. We said no thank you, because just from watching, Winter had to crawl between the empty gun mounts and retch at length but in vain in the direction of the harbour mouth.

After this bit of conspicuous consumption, Mahlke naturally received his portion of applause; waving it aside, he fed the putrid corned beef and what was left of the frogs' legs to the gulls which had been coming steadily closer during his banquet. Finally he bowled the tins and shooed the gulls overboard, and scoured the opener which alone struck him as worth keeping. From then on he wore the tin opener suspended from his neck by a string like the English screwdriver and his various amulets, but not regularly, only when he was planning to look for tinned food in the galley of a former Polish mine sweeper – his stomach never seemed to mind. On such days he came to school with the can opener under his shirt beside the rest of his ironmongery; he even wore it to early Mass in St Mary's Chapel; for whenever Mahlke knelt at the altar rail, tilting his head back and sticking out his tongue for Father Gusewski to lay the Host on, the altar boy by the priest's side would peer into Mahlke's shirt collar: and there, dangling from your neck was the opener, side by side with the Madonna and the grease-coated screwdriver; and I admired you, though you were not trying to arouse my admiration. No, Mahlke never made much of an effort in that direction.

In the autumn of the same year in which he had learned to swim, they threw him out of the Young Folk and into the Hitler Youth, because several Sundays in a row he had refused to lead his squad – he was a squad leader in the Young Folk – to the morning meet in Jeschkenthal Forest. That too, in our class at least, brought him out-spoken admiration. He received our enthusiasm with the usual mixture of coolness and embarrassment and con-tinued, now as a rank-and-file member of the Hitler Youth, to shirk his duty on Sunday mornings; but in this organiza-tion, which embraced the whole male population from fourteen to twenty, his remissness attracted less attention, for the Hitler Youth was not as strict as the Young Folk, it was a big, sprawling organization in which fellows like Mahlke could blend with their surroundings. Besides, he wasn't insubordinate in the usual sense; he regularly attended the training sessions during the week, made himself useful in the 'special activities' that were scheduled more and more frequently, and was glad to help with the junk collections or stand on street corners with a Winter Aid tin, as long as it didn't interfere with his early Mass on Sunday. There was nothing unusual about being trans-ferred from the Young Folk to the Hitler Youth, and

Member Mahlke remained a colourless unknown quantity in the official youth organization, while in our school, after the first summer on the barge, his reputation, though neither good nor bad, became legendary.

There is no doubt that unlike the Hitler Youth our gymnasium became for you, in the long run, a source of high hopes which no common gymnasium, with its traditional mixture of rigour and good fellowship, with its coloured school caps and its often invoked school spirit could possibly fulfil.

'What's the matter with him?'

'I think he's a bit touched.'

'Maybe it's got something to do with his father's death.'

'And what about all that ironmongery on his neck?'

'And he's always running off to pray.'

'And he doesn't believe in anything if you ask me.'

'Not likely, he's too realistic.'

'And what about that thing on his neck?'

'You ask him, you're the one that stuck the cat on him. . . . '

We racked our brains and we couldn't understand you. Before you could swim, you were a nobody, who was called on now and then, usually gave correct answers, and was named Joachim Mahlke. And yet I believe that in Sixth or maybe it was later, certainly before your first attempts at swimming, we sat on the same bench; or you sat behind me or in the same row in the middle section, while I sat behind Schilling near the window. Later somebody recollected that you had worn glasses up to Fifth Form; I never noticed them. I didn't even notice those eternal laced boots of yours until you had made the grade with your swimming and begun to wear a bootlace round your neck. Great events were shaking the world just then, but Mahlke's time reckoning was Before learning to swim and After learning to swim; for when the war broke out

26

all over the place, not all at once but little by little, first on the Westerplatte, then on the radio, then in the newspapers, this schoolboy who could neither swim nor ride a bicycle didn't amount to much; but the mine sweeper of the *Czaika* class, which was later to provide him with his first chance to perform, was already, if only for a few weeks, playing its military role in the Pitziger Wiek, in the Gulf, and in the fishing port of Hela.

The Polish fleet was small but ambitious. We knew its modern ships, for the most part built in England or France, by heart, and could reel off their guns, tonnage, and speed in knots with never a mistake, just as we could recite the names of all Italian light cruisers, or of all the obsolete Brazilian battleships and monitors.

Later Mahlke took the lead also in this branch of knowledge; he learned to pronounce fluently and without hesitation the names of the Japanese destroyers from the modern *Kasumi* class, built in '38, to the slower craft of the *Asagao* class, modernized in '23: *Fumizuki, Satsuki Yuuzuki, Hokaze, Nadakaze* and *Oite*.

It didn't take very long to rattle off the units of the Polish fleet. There were the two destroyers, the *Blyskawica* and the *Grom*, two thousand tons thirty-eight knots, but they decommissioned themselves two days before the outbreak of the war, put into English ports, and were incorporated into the British Navy. The *Blyskawica* is still in existence. She has been converted into a floating naval museum in Gdynia and school teachers take their classes to see it.

The destroyer *Burza*, fifteen hundred tons, thirty-three knots, took the same trip to England. Of the five Polish submarines, only the *Wilk* and, after an adventurous journey without maps or captain, the eleven hundred ton *Orzel* succeeded in reaching English ports. The *Rys, Zbik,* and *Semp* allowed themselves to be interned in Sweden.

By the time the war broke out, the ports of Gdynia,

Putzig, Heisternest and Hela were bereft of naval vessels except for an obsolete former French cruiser which served as a training ship and dormitory, the mine layer *Gryf*, built in the Norman Dockyards of Le Havre, a heavily armed vessel of two thousand tons, carrying three hundred mines. Otherwise there were a lone destroyer, the *Wicher*, a few former German torpedo boats, and the six mine sweepers of the *Czaika* class, which also laid mines. These last had a speed of eighteen knots; their armament consisted of a 75 millimetre forward gun and four machine-guns on revolving mounts; they carried, so the official handbooks say, a complement of twenty mines.

And one of these one hundred and eighty-five ton vessels had been built specially for Mahlke.

The naval battle in the Gulf of Danzig lasted from the first of September to the second of October. The score, after the capitulation on Hela Peninsula, was as follows: The Polish units *Gryf*, *Wicher*, *Baltyk*, as well as the three mine sweepers of the *Czaika* class, the *Mewa*, the *Jaskolko*, and the *Czapla* had been destroyed by fire and sunk in their ports; the German destroyer *Leberecht* had been damaged by artillery fire, the mine sweeper *M85* ran into a Polish anti-submarine mine north of Heisternest and lost a third of her crew.

Only the remaining, slightly damaged vessels of the *Czaika* class were captured. The *Zuraw* and the *Czaika* were soon commissioned under the names of *Oxthöft* and *Westerplatte*; as the third, the *Rybitwa*, was being towed from Hela to Neufahrwasser, it began to leak, settle, and wait for Joachim Mahlke; for it was he who in the following summer raised brass plaques on which the name *Rybitwa* had been engraved. Later, it was said that a Polish officer and a bosun's mate, obliged to man the rudder under German guard, had flooded the barge in accordance with the well-known Scapa Flow recipe.

For some reason or other it sank to one side of the

channel, not far from the Neufahrwasser harbour buoy and, though it lay conveniently on one of the many sandbanks, was not salvaged, but spent the rest of the war right there, with only its bridge, the remains of its rail, its battered ventilators, and forward gun mount (the gun itself had been removed) emerging from the water – a strange sight at first, but soon a familiar one. It provided you, Joachim Mahlke, with a goal in life; just as the battleship *Gneisenau*, which was sunk in February' 45 just outside of Gdynia harbour, became a goal for Polish schoolboys; though I can only wonder whether among the Polish boys who dived and looted the *Gneisenau*, there was any who took to the water with the same fanaticism as Mahlke.

Chapter Three

He was not a thing of beauty. He could have had his Adam's apple repaired. Possibly that piece of cartilage was the whole trouble.

But it went with the rest of him. Besides, you can't prove everything by proportions. And as for his soul, it was never introduced to me. I never heard what he thought. In the end, all I really had to go by was his neck and its numerous counterweights. It is true that he took enormous bundles of margarine sandwiches to school and to the beach with him and would devour quantities of them just before going into the water. But this can only be taken as one more reminder of his mouse, for the mouse chewed insatiably.

There were also his devotions at the altar of the Virgin. He took no particular interest in the Crucified One. It struck me that though the bobbing on his neck did not cease when he joined his fingertips in prayer, he swallowed in slow motion on these occasions and contrived, by

29

arranging his hands in an exaggeratedly stylized pose, to distract attention from that elevator above his shirt collar and his pendants on strings, bootlaces and chains – which never stopped running.

Apart from the Virgin he didn't have much truck with girls. Maybe if he had had a sister. My girl cousins weren't much use to him either. His relations with Tulla Pokriefke don't count, they were an anomaly and would not have been bad as a circus act – remember, he was planning to become a clown – for Tulla, a spindly little thing with legs like toothpicks, might just as well have been a boy. In any case, this scrawny girl child who swam along with us when she felt like it during our second summer on the barge, was never the least embarrassed when we decided to give our swimming trunks a rest and sprawled naked on the rusty bridge, with very little idea what to do with ourselves.

You can draw a good likeness of Tulla's face with the most familiar punctuation marks. The way she glided through the water, she might have had webs between her toes. Always, even on the barge, despite seaweed, gulls, and the sour smell of the rust, she stank of carpenter's glue, because her father worked with glue in her uncle's carpenter's shop. She was all skin, bones, and curiosity. Calmly, her chin in the cup of her hand, Tulla would look on when Winter or Esch, unable to contain himself, produced his modest offerings. Hunching over so that the bones of her spine stuck out, she would gaze at Winter who was always slow in getting there, and mutter: 'You're certainly taking a long time!'

But when finally it splashed on the rust, she would begin to fidget and squirm, she would throw herself down on her belly, make little rat's eyes and look and look, trying to discover heaven-knows-what, turn over, sit up, rise to her knees and her feet, stand slightly knock-kneed over the wetness, and begin to stir it with a supple big toe,

30

until it foamed rust-red: 'That's a good 'un. Now you do it, Atze.'

Tulla never wearied of this little game – yes, game, the whole thing was all perfectly innocent. 'Aw, you do it,' she would plead in that whining voice of hers. 'Who hasn't done it yet? It's your turn.'

She always found some good-natured fool who would get to work even if he wasn't at all in the mood, just to give her something to goggle at. The only one who wouldn't do it until Tulla found the right words of encouragement – and that is why I am narrating these heroic deeds – was the great swimmer and diver Joachim Mahlke. While all the rest of us were engaging in this time-honoured, nay Biblical, pursuit, either one at a time or – as the manual puts it – with others, together, Mahlke kept his trunks on and gazed fixedly in the direction of Hela. We felt certain that at home, in his room between snowy owl and Sistine Madonna, he indulged in the same sport.

He had just come up, shivering as usual, and he had nothing to show. Schilling had just been working for Tulla. A coaster was entering the harbour under her own power. 'Do it again,' Tulla begged, for Schilling was the most prolific of all. Not a single ship in the roadstead. 'Not after swimming. I'll do it again tomorrow,' Schilling consoled her. Tulla turned on her heel and stood with outspread toes facing Mahlke, who as usual was shivering in the shadow of the pilot house and hadn't sat down yet. A high seas tug with a forward gun was putting out to sea.

'Won't you? Aw, do it just once. Or can't you? Don't you want to? Or aren't you allowed to?'

Mahlke stepped half out of the shadow and slapped Tulla's compressed little face left right with his palm and the back of his hand. His mouse went wild. So did the screwdriver. Tulla, of course, didn't shed one single tear, but gave a bleating laugh with her mouth closed; shaking

31

with laughter, she arched her india-rubber frame effortlessly into a bridge, and peered through her spindly legs at Mahlke until he – he was back in the shade again and the tug was veering off to northwestward – said: 'OK. Just so you'll shut up.'

Tulla came out of her contortion and squatted down normally with her legs folded under her, as Mahlke stripped his trunks down to his knees. The children at the Punch and Judy show gaped in amazement: a few deft movements emanating from his right wrist, and his member loomed so large that the tip emerged from the shadow of the pilot house and the sun fell on it. Only when we had all formed a semicircle did Mahlke's jumping Jim return to the shadow.

'Won't you let me just for a second?' Tulla's mouth hung open. Mahlke nodded and dropped his right hand, though without uncurving his fingers. Tulla's hand, scratched and bruised as they always were, approached the monster, which expanded under her questioning fingertips; the veins stood out and the glans protruded.

'Measure it!' cried Jürgen Kupka. Tulla spread the fingers of her left hand. One full span and another almost. Somebody and then somebody else whispered: 'At least twelve inches!' That was an exaggeration of course. Schilling, who otherwise had the longest, had to take his out, make it stand up, and hold it beside Mahlke's: Mahlke's was first of all a size thicker, second a matchbox longer, and third looked much more grown-up, dangerous, and worthy to be worshipped.

He had shown us again, and then a second time he showed us by producing not one but two mighty streams in quick succession. With his knees not quite together, Mahlke stood by the twisted rail beside the pilot house, staring out in the direction of the harbour buoy, a little to the rear of the low-lying smoke of the vanishing high-seas tug; a torpedo-boat of the *Gull* class was just emerging from the harbour, but he didn't let it distract him. Thus he stood, showing his profile, from the toes extending just over the edge to the watershed in the middle of his hair: strangely enough, the length of his sexual part made up for the otherwise shocking protuberance of his Adam's apple, lending his body an odd, but in its way perfect harmony.

No sooner had Mahlke finished squirting the first load over the rail than he started in all over again. Winter timed him with his watertight wrist watch; Mahlke's performance continued for approximately as many seconds as it took the torpedo boat to pass from the tip of the breakwater to the buoy; then, while the torpedo boat was rounding the buoy, he unloaded the same amount again; the foaming bubbles lurched in the smooth, only occasionally rippling swell, and we laughed for joy as the gulls swooped down, screaming for more.

Joachim Mahlke was never obliged to repeat or better this performance, for none of us ever touched his record, certainly not when exhausted from swimming and diving; sportsmen in everything we did, we respected the rules.

For a while Tulla Pokriefke, for whom his prowess must have had the most direct appeal, courted him in her way; she would always be sitting by the pilot house, staring at Mahlke's swimming trunks. A few times she pleaded with him, but he always refused, though good-naturedly.

'Do you have to confess these things?'

Mahlke nodded, and played with his dangling screw-driver to divert her gaze.

'Well you take me down some time? By myself I'm scared. I bet there's still a corpse down there.'

For educational purposes, no doubt, Mahlke took Tulla down into the fo'c'sle. He kept her under much too long. When they came up, she had turned a greyish yellow

33

and sagged in his arms. We had to stand her light, curveless body on its head.

After that Tulla Pokriefke didn't join us very often and, though she was more regular than other girls of her age, she got increasingly on our nerves with her drivel about the dead sailor in the barge. She was always going on about him. 'The one that brings him up,' she promised 'can-you-know-what.'

It is perfectly possible that without admitting it to ourselves we all searched. Mahlke in the engine room, the rest of us in the fo'c'sle, for a half-decomposed Polish sailor not because we really wanted to lay this unfinished little number, but just so.

Yet even Mahlke found nothing except for a few half-rotted pieces of clothing, from which fishes darted until the gulls saw that something was stirring and began to say grace.

No, he didn't set much store by Tulla, though they say there was something between them later. He didn't go for girls, not even for Schilling's sister. And all my cousins from Berlin got out of him was a fishy stare. If he had any tender feelings at all, it was for boys; by which I don't mean to suggest that Mahlke was queer; in those years spent between the beach and the sunken barge, we none of us knew exactly whether we were male or female. Though later there may have been rumours and tangible evidence to the contrary, the fact is that the only woman Mahlke cared about was the Catholic Virgin Mary. It was for her sake alone that he dragged everything that can be worn and displayed on the human neck to St Mary's Chapel. Whatever he did, from diving to his subsequent military accomplishments, was done for her or else – yes, I know, I'm contradicting myself again – to distract attention from his Adam's apple. And perhaps, in addition to Virgin and mouse, there was yet a third motive: Our school, that musty edifice that defied ventilation, and particularly the auditorium, meant a great deal to Joachim Mahlke; it was the school that drove you, later on, to your supreme effort.

And now it is time to say something about Mahlke's face. A few of us have survived the war; we live in small small towns and large small towns, we've gained weight and lost hair, and we more or less earn our living. I saw Schilling in Duisburg and Jürgen Kupka in Braunschweig shortly before he emigrated to Canada. Both of them started right in about the Adam's apple. 'My God – that thing on his throat! And remember that time with the cat. Wasn't it you that put the cat on him. . . . ' and I had to interrupt: 'That's not what I'm after; it's his face I'm interested in.'

We agreed as a starter that he had grey or grey-blue eyes, bright but not shining, anyway that they were not brown. The face thin and rather elongated, muscular around the cheek bones. The nose not strikingly large, but fleshy, quickly reddening in cold weather. His overhanging occiput has already been mentioned. We had difficulty in coming to an agreement about Mahlke's upper lip. Jürgen Kupka was of my opinion that it curled up and never wholly covered his two upper incisors, which in turn were not vertical but stuck out like tusks – except of course when he was diving. But then we began to have our doubts; we remembered that the little Pokriefke girl also had a curled-up lip and always visible incisors. In the end we weren't sure whether we hadn't mixed up Mahlke and Tulla, though just in connexion with the upper lip. Maybe it was only she whose lip was that way, for hers was, that much is certain. In Duisburg Schilling – we met in the station restaurant, because his wife had some objection to unannounced visitors – reminded me of the caricature that had created an uproar in our class for several days. In '41 I think it was, a big, tall character turned up in our class, who had been evacuated from Latvia with his family. In spite of his cracked voice, he was a fluent talker; an aristocrat, always fashionably dressed, knew Greek, lectured like a book, his father was a baron, wore a fur cap in the winter, what *was* his name? – well, anyway, his first name was Karel. And he could draw, very quickly, with or without models: sleighs surrounded by wolves, drunken Cossacks, Jews like in *Der Stürmer*, naked girls riding on lions, in general lots of naked girls with long porcelain-like legs, but never smutty, Bolsheviks devouring babies, Hitler disguised as Charlemagne, racing cars driven by ladies with long flowing scarves; and he was especially clever at drawing caricatures of his teachers or fellow students with pen, brush, or crayon on every available scrap of paper or with chalk on the blackboard; well, he didn't do Mahlke on paper, but with rasping chalk on the blackboard.

He drew him full face. At that time Mahlke already had his ridiculous parting in the middle, fixed with sugar water. He represented the face as a triangle with one corner at the chin. The mouth was puckered and peevish. No trace of any visible incisors that might have been mistaken for tusks. The eyes, piercing points under sorrowfully uplifted eyebrows. The neck sinuous, half in profile with a monstrous Adam's apple. And behind the head and sorrowful features a halo: a perfect likeness of Mahlke the Redeemer. The effect was immediate.

We snorted and whinnied on our benches and only recovered our senses when someone set about the handsome Karel So-and-so, first with his bare fists, then, just before we managed to separate them, with a steel screwdriver.

It was I who sponged your Redeemer's countenance off the blackboard.

36

Chapter Four

With and without irony: maybe you wouldn't have become a clown but some sort of creator of fashions; for it was Mahlke who during the winter after the second summer on the barge created the pompoms: two little woollen spheres the size of pingpong balls, in solid or mixed colours, attached to a plaited woollen cord that was worn under the collar like a necklace and tied into a bow so that the two pompoms hung at an angle, more or less like a bow tie. I have checked and am able to state authoritatively that beginning in the third winter of the war, the pompoms came to be worn almost all over Germany, but mostly in northern and eastern Germany, particularly by high school students. It was Mahlke who introduced them to our school. He might have invented them. And maybe he actually did. He had several pairs made according to his specifications by his Aunt Susi mostly from the frayed yarn unravelled from his dead father's much darned socks. Then he wore the first pair to school and they were very very conspicuous on his neck.

Then days later they were in the drapers' shops, at first in cardboard boxes bashfully tucked away by the cash register, but soon attractively displayed in the showcases. An important factor in their success was that they could be had without coupons. From Langfuhr they spread triumphantly through eastern and northern Germany; they were worn – I have witnesses to bear me out – even in Leipzig, in Pirna, and months later, after Mahlke had discarded his own, a few isolated pairs made their appearance as far west as the Rhineland and the Palatinate. I remember the exact day when Mahlke removed his invention from his neck and will speak of it in due time.

We wore the pompoms for several months, toward the end as a protest, after Dr Klohse, our principal, had branded this article of apparel as effeminate and unworthy of a German young man, and forbidden us to wear pompoms inside the school building or even in the recreation yard. Klohse's order was read in all the classrooms, but there were many who complied only during actual classes. The pompoms remind me of Papa Brunies, a pensioned teacher who had been recalled to his post during the war; he was delighted with the merry little things; once or twice, after Mahlke had given them up, he even tied a pair of them around his own standup collar, and thus attired declaimed Eichendorff: 'Weathered gables, lofty windows . . . ' or maybe it was something else, but in any case it was Eichendorff, his favourite poet – Oswald Brunies had a sweet tooth and later, ostensibly because he had eaten some vitamin tablets that were supposed to be distributed among the students, but probably for political reasons – Brunies was a Freemason – he was arrested at school. Some of the students were questioned. I hope I didn't testify against him. His adoptive daughter, a doll-like creature who took ballet lessons, wore mourning in public; they took him to Stutthof, and there he stayed – a dismal, complicated story, which deserves to be written, but somewhere else, not by me, and certainly not in connexion with Mahlke.

Let's get back to the pompoms. Of course Mahlke had invented them to make things easier for his Adam's apple. For a time they quieted the unruly jumping-jack, but when the pompoms came into style all over the place, even in the Sixth Form, they ceased to attract attention on their inventor's neck. I can still see Mahlke during the winter of '42 – which must have been hard for him because diving was out and the pompoms had lost their efficacy – always in monumental solitude, striding in his black boots, down Osterzeile and up Bärenweg to St Mary's Chapel, over crunching cinder-strewn snow. Hatless. Ears, red, brittle, and prominent. Hair stiff with sugar water and frost, parted in the middle from crown to forehead. Brows knitted in anguish. Horror-stricken, watery-blue eyes that see more than is there. Turned-up coat collar. The coat had also come down to him from his late father. A grey woollen scarf, crossed under his tapering to scrawny chin, was held in place, as could be seen from a distance, by a safety pin. Every twenty paces his right hand rises from his coat pocket to feel whether his scarf is still in place, properly protecting his neck – I have seen clowns, Grock in the circus, Charlie Chaplin in the movies, working with the same gigantic safety pin. Mahlke is practising: men, women, soldiers on furlough, children, singly and in groups, grow toward him over the snow. Their breath, Mahlke's too, puffs up white from their mouths and vanishes over their shoulders. And the eyes of all who approach him are focused, Mahlke is probably thinking on that comical, very comical, excruciatingly comical safety pin.

In the same dry, hard winter I arranged an expedition over the frozen sea to the ice-bound mine sweeper with my two girl cousins, who had come from Berlin for Christmas vacation, and Schilling to make things come out even. The girls were pretty, sleek, tousled blonde, and spoiled from living in Berlin. We thought we would show off a bit and impress them with our barge. The girls were awfully ladylike in the tram and even on the beach, but out there we were hoping to do something really wild with them, we didn't know what.

Mahlke ruined our afternoon. In opening up the harbour channel, the ice breakers had pushed great boulders of ice toward the barge: jammed together, they piled up into a fissured wall, which sang as the wind blew over it and hid part of the barge from view. We caught sight of

Mahlke only when we had mounted the ice barrier, which was about as tall as we were, and had pulled the girls up after us. The bridge, the pilot house, the ventilators aft of the bridge, and whatever else had remained above water formed a single chunk of glazed, bluish-white candy, licked ineffectually by a congealed sun. No gulls. They were farther out, over the garbage of some ice-bound freighters in the roadstead.

Of course Mahlke had turned up his coat collar and tied his scarf, with the safety pin out in front, under his chin. No hat, but round, black ear-muffs, such as those worn by dustmen and the drivers of brewers' drays, covered his otherwise protruding ears, joined by a strip of metal at right angles to the parting in his hair.

He was so hard at work on the sheet of ice over the bow that he didn't notice us; he even seemed to be keeping warm. He was trying with a small axe to cut through the ice at a point which he presumed to be directly over the open forward hatch. With quick short strokes he was making a circular groove, about the size of a manhole cover. Schilling and I jumped from the wall, caught the girls, and introduced them to him. No gloves to take off; he merely shifted the axe to his left hand. Each of us in turn received a prickly-hot right hand, and a moment later he was chopping again. Both girls had their mouths slightly open. Little teeth grew cold. Frosty breath beat against their scarves and frosty-eyed they stared at his ice-cutting operations. Schilling and I were through. But though furious with him, we began to tell about his summertime accomplishments as a diver: 'Metal plates, absolutely, and a fire extinguisher, and tin cans, he opened them right up and guess what was in them – human flesh! And when he brought up the gramophone something came crawling out of it, and one time he . . . '

The girls didn't quite follow, they asked stupid questions, and addressed Mahlke as Mister. He kept right on hacking. He shook his head and ear-muffs as we shouted his diving prowess over the ice, but never forgot to feel for his muffler and safety pin with his free hand. When we could think of nothing more to say and were just standing there shivering, he would stop for a moment every twenty strokes or so, though without ever standing up quite straight, and fill the pause with simple, modest explanations. Embarrassed, but at the same time self-assured, he dwelt on his lesser exploits and passed over the more daring feats, speaking more of his work than of adventures in the moist interior of the sunken mine sweeper. In the meantime he drove his groove deeper and deeper into the ice. I wouldn't say that my cousins were exactly fascinated by Mahlke; no, he wasn't witty enough for that and his choice of words was too commonplace. Besides, such little ladies would never have gone all out for anybody wearing black ear-muffs like a grandpa. Nevertheless, we were through. He turned us into shivering little boys with running noses, standing there definitely on the edge of things; and even on the way back the girls treated us with condescension.

Mahlke stayed on; he wanted to finish cutting his hole, to prove to himself that he had correctly figured the spot over the hatch. He didn't ask us to wait till he had finished, but he did delay our departure for a good five minutes when we were already on top of the wall, by dispensing a series of words in an undertone, not at us, more in the direction of the ice-bound freighters in the roadstead.

Still chopping, he asked us to help him. Or was it an order, politely spoken? In any case he wanted us to make water in the wedge-shaped groove, so as to melt or at least soften the ice with warm urine. Before Schilling or I could say: 'Not, likely,' or 'We just did,' my little cousins piped up joyfully: 'Oh yes, we'd love to. But you must turn your backs, and you too, Mr Mahlke.'

After Mahlke had explained where they should squat

41

– the whole stream, he said, has to fall in the same place or it won't do any good – he climbed upon the wall and turned toward the beach. While amid whispering and tittering the sprinkler duet went on behind us, we concentrated on the swarms of black ants near Brösen and on the icy pier. The seventeen poplars on the Beach Promenade were coated with sugar. The golden globe at the tip of the Soldiers' Monument, an obelisk towering over Brösen Park, blinked at us excitedly. Sunday all over.

When the girls' ski pants had been pulled up again and we stood round the groove with the tips of our shoes, the circle was still steaming, especially in the two places where Mahlke had cut crosses with his axe. The water stood pale-yellow in the ditch and seeped away with a crackling sound. The edges of the grooves were tinged a golden green. The ice sang plaintively. A pungent smell persisted because there were no other smells to counteract it, growing stronger as Mahlke chopped some more at the groove and scraped away about as much slush as a common bucket might have held. Especially in the two marked spots, he succeeded in drilling shafts, in gaining depth.

The soft ice was piled up to one side and began at once to crust over in the cold. Then he marked two new places. When the girls had turned away, we unbuttoned and helped Mahlke by thawing an inch or two more of the ice and boring two fresh holes. But they were still not deep enough. He himself did not pass water, and we didn't ask him to; on the contrary we were afraid the girls might try to encourage him.

As soon as we had finished and before my cousins could say a word, Mahlke sent us away. We looked back from the wall; he had pushed up muffler and safety pin over his chin and nose; his neck was still covered but now his pompoms, white sprinkled red, were taking the air between muffler and coat collar. He was hacking again at his groove which was whispering something or other about the girls and us – a bowed form barely discernible through floating veils of sun-stirred laundry steam.

On the way back to Brösen, the conversation was all about him. Alternately or both at once, my cousins asked questions. We didn't always have the answer. But when the younger one wanted to know why Mahlke wore his muffler so high up and the other one started in on the muffler too, Schilling seized on the opportunity and described Mahlke's Adam's apple, giving it all the qualities of a goitre. He made exaggerated swallowing motions, imitated Mahlke chewing, took off his ski cap, gave his hair a kind of parting in the middle with his fingers, and finally succeeded in making the girls laugh at Mahlke; they even said he was an odd chap and not quite right in the head.

But despite this little triumph at your expense – I put in my two cents' worth too, mimicking your relations with the Virgin Mary – we made no headway with my cousins beyond the usual necking in the movies. And a week later they returned to Berlin.

Here I am bound to report that the following day I rode out to Brösen bright and early; I ran across the ice through a dense coastal fog, almost missing the barge, and found the hole over the fo'c'sle completed. During the night a fresh crust of ice had formed; with considerable difficulty, I broke through it with the heel of my shoe and an iron-tipped cane belonging to my father, which I had brought along for that very purpose. Then I poked the cane around through the cracked ice in the grey-black hole. It disappeared almost to the handle, water splashed my glove; and then the tip struck the deck, no, not the deck, it jutted into empty space. It was only when I moved the cane sideways along the edge of the hole that it met resistance.

43

And I passed iron over iron: the hole was directly over the open forward hatch. Exactly like one plate under another in a pile of plates, the hatch was right under the hole in the ice – well no, that's an exaggeration, not *exactly*, there's no such thing: either the hatch was a little bigger or the hole was a little bigger; but the fit was pretty good, and my pride in Joachim Mahlke was as sweet as chocolate creams. I'd have liked to give you my wrist watch.

I stayed there a good ten minutes; I sat on the circular mound of ice – it must have been all of eighteen inches high. The lower third was marked with a pale yellow ring of urine from the day before. It had been our privilege to help him. But even without our help Mahlke would have finished his hole. Was it possible that he could manage without an audience? Were there shows he put on only for himself? For not even the gulls would have admired your hole in the ice over the forward hatch, if I hadn't gone out there to admire you.

He always had an audience. When I say that always, even while cutting his circular groove over the ice-bound barge, he had the Virgin Mary behind or before him, that she looked with enthusiasm upon his little axe, the Church shouldn't really object; but even if the Church refuses to put up with the idea of a Virgin Mary forever engaged in admiring Mahlke's exploits, the fact remains that she always watched him attentively: I know. For I was an altar boy, first under Father Wiehnke at the Church of the Sacred Heart, then under Gusewski at St Mary's Chapel. I kept on assisting him at Mass long after I had lost my faith in the magic of the altar, a process which approximately coincided with my growing up. The comings and goings amused me. I took pains too. I didn't shuffle like most altar boys. The truth is, I was never sure and to this day I am not sure, whether there might not after all be something behind or in front of the altar or in the tabernacle. . . . At any rate Father Gusewski was always glad to have me as one of his two altar boys, because I never swapped cigarette cards between offering and consecration, never rang the bells too loud or too long, or made a business of selling the sacramental wine. For altar boys are holy terrors: not only do they spread out the usual juvenile trinkets on the altar steps; not only do they lay bets, payable in coins or worn-out ball bearings – Oh no. Even during the gradual prayers they discuss the technical details of the world's warships, sunk or afloat, and substitute snatches of such lore for the words of the Mass, or smuggle them in between Latin and Latin: *'Introibo ad altare Dei* – say, when was the cruiser *Eritrea* launched ? – '36. Special features ? – *Ad Deum, qui laetificat juventutem meam.* – Only Italian cruiser in East African waters. Displacement ? – *Deus fortitudo mea* – 2172 tons. Speed ? – *Et introibo ad altare Dei* – Search me. Armament ? – *Sicut erat in principio* – six 150-millimetre guns, four seventy fives. . . . Wrong! – *et nunc et semper* – No, it's right. Names of the German artillery training ships ? – *et in saecula saeculorum, Amen.* – *Brummer* and *Bremse.'*

Later on I stopped serving regularly at St Mary's and came only when Gusewski sent for me because his boys were busy with Sunday hikes or collecting funds for Winter Aid.

I'm telling you all this only to explain my presence at the main altar, for from there I was able to observe Mahlke as he knelt at the altar of the Virgin. My, how he could pray! That calf-like look. His eyes would grow steadily glassier. His mouth peevish, perpetually moving without punctuation. Fishes tossed up on the beach gasp for air with the same regularity. I shall try to give you an idea of how relentlessly Mahlke could pray. Father Gusewski was distributing communion. When he came to Mahlke, who always, seen from the altar, knelt at the outer left, this particular kneeler was one who had forgotten all caution, allowing his muffler and gigantic safety pin to shift for themselves, whose eyes had congealed, whose head and parted hair were tilted backward, who allowed his tongue to hang out, and who, in this attitude, left an agitated mouse so exposed and defenceless that I might have caught it in my hand. But perhaps Joachim Mahlke realized that his cynosure was convulsed and exposed. Perhaps he intentionally accentuated its frenzy with exaggerated swallowing, in order to attract the glass eyes of the Virgin standing to one side of him; for I cannot and will not believe that you ever did anything whatsoever without an audience.

Chapter Five

I never saw him with pompoms at St Mary's Chapel. Although the style was just beginning to catch on, he wore them less and less. Sometimes when three of us were standing in the recreation yard, always under the same chestnut tree, all talking at once over our bits of woollen nonsense, Mahlke removed his pompoms from his neck; then, after the second bell had rung, he would tie them on again, irresolutely, for lack of a better counterweight.

When for the first time a graduate of our school returned from the front, a special bell signal called us to the auditorium though classes were still in progress. On the return journey he had stopped briefly at the Führer's Headquarters, and now he had the coveted lozenge on his neck. He stood, not behind but beside the old brown pulpit, at the end of the hall, against a background of three tall windows, a row of potted leafy plants, and the faculty gathered into a semicircle. Lozenge on neck, red rosebud mouth, he projected his voice into the space over our heads and made little explanatory gestures. Mahlke was sitting in the row ahead of me and Schilling. I saw his ears turn a flaming transparent red; he leaned back stiffly, and I saw him, left right, fiddling with something on his neck, tugging, gagging and at length tossing something under his bench: something woollen, pompoms, a green and red mixture I think they were. The young fellow, a lieutenant in the Air Force, started off hesitantly and rather too softly, with an appealing awkwardness; he even blushed once or twice, though there was nothing in what he was saying to warrant it: ' . . . well, boys, don't get the idea that life in the Air Force is like a rabbit hunt, all action and never a dull moment. Sometimes nothing happens for whole weeks. But when they sent us to the Channel, I says to myself, if things don't start popping now, they never will. And I was right. On the very first mission a formation with a fighter escort came straight at us, and believe me, it was a real merry-go-round. In and out of the clouds, winding and circling the whole time. I try to gain altitude, down below me there's three Spitfires circling, trying to hide in the clouds. I says to myself, it's just too bad if I can't . . . I dive, I've got him in my sights, bam, he's trailing smoke. Just time to turn over on my left wing tip when there's a second Spitfire coming toward me in my sights, I go straight for his nose, it's him or me; well, as you can see, it's him that went into the drink, and I says to myself, as long as you've got two, why not try the third and so on, as long as your fuel holds out. So I see seven of them down below me, they've broken formation and they're trying to get away. I pick out one of them, I've got a good sun behind me. He gets his lot, I repeat the number, turns out OK, I pull back the stick as far as she'll go, and there's the third in my line of fire: he goes into a spin, I must have got him, instinctively I trail him, lose him, clouds, got him again, give another burst, he drops into the pond, but so do I pretty near; I

47

honestly can't tell you how I got my crate upstairs again. Anyway, when I come home flapping my wings – as you probably know, you must have seen it in the newsreels, we come in flapping our wings if we've bagged anything – I can't get the landing gear down. Jammed. So I had to make my first crash landing. Later in the officers' club they tell me I've been marked up for a certain six, it's news to me; as you can imagine, I'd been too excited to count. I was pretty pleased, but about four o'clock we've got to go up again. Well, to make a long story short, it was pretty much the same as in the old days when we played handball in our good old recreation yard – 'cause the stadium hadn't been built yet. Maybe Mr Mallenbrandt remembers: either I didn't shoot a single goal or I'd shoot nine in a row; that's how it was that day: six that morning and three more in the afternoon. That was my ninth to seventeenth; but it wasn't until a good six months later, when I had my full forty, that I was commended by our CO, and by the time I was decorated at the Führer's headquarters, I had forty-four under my belt; 'cause we fellows up at the Channel just about lived in our crates. The ground crews got relieved, not us. There were some that couldn't take it. Well, now I'll tell you something funny for relief. In every airfield there's a squadron dog. One day it was beautiful weather and we decided to take Alex, our dog . . .'

Such, approximately, were the words of the gloriously decorated lieutenant. In between two air battles, as an interlude, he told the story of Alex, the squadron dog, who had been compelled to learn parachute jumping. There was also the little anecdote about the corporal who was always too slow in getting up when the alert was sounded and was obliged to fly several missions in his pyjamas.

The lieutenant laughed with his audience; even the graduating class laughed, and some of the teachers indulged in a chuckle. He had graduated from our school in '33 and was shot down over the Ruhr in '43. His hair was dark-brown, unparted, combed rigorously back; he wasn't very big, looked rather like a dapper little waiter in a night club. While speaking he kept one hand in his pocket, but took it out whenever he needed two hands to illustrate an air battle with. His use of his outspread palms was subtle and masterful; with a twist of his shoulders, he could make you see his plane banking as it circled in quest of victims, and he had no need of long, explanatory sentences. His chopped phrases were more like cues for his pantomime. At the height of his act he roared out engine noises or stuttered when an engine was in trouble. It was safe to assume that he had practised his number in his airfield officers' mess, especially as the word mess kept cropping up in his narrative: 'We were sitting peacefully in the mess . . . I was just heading for the mess 'cause I wanted to . . . In our mess there's a . . . ' But even aside from his mime's hands and his realistic sound effects, he knew how to appeal to his audience; he managed, for instance, to get in a few cracks at some of our teachers who still had the same nicknames as in his days. But he was always pleasant, full of harmless mischief. And no boaster. He never claimed credit for the difficult things he had done, but put everything down to his luck: 'I've always been lucky, even in school, when I think of some of my report cards . . . ' And in the middle of a schoolboy's joke he suddenly remembered three or four classmates who, as he said, shall not have died in vain. He concluded his talk not with the names of the three dead comrades, but with his naïve, heartfelt admission: 'Boys, let me tell you this: every single one of us who's out there fighting likes to think about his schooldays and, believe me, we often do.'

We clapped, roared and stamped at great length. Only when my hands were hot and burning did I observe that Mahlke was holding back and contributing no applause.

Up in front Dr Klohse shook both his former student's hands demonstratively as long as the applause went on. Then after gripping the frail figure for a moment by the shoulders, he turned abruptly away, and took up his stance behind the pulpit, while the lieutenant quickly sat down.

The principal's speech went on and on. Boredom spread from the lush green plants to the oil painting on the rear wall of the auditorium, a portrait of Baron von Conradi the founder of our school. Even the lieutenant, a slender figure between Brunies and Mallenbrandt, kept looking at his fingernails. In this lofty hall Klohse's cool peppermint breath, which suffused all his mathematics classes, substituting for the odour of pure science, wasn't much of a help. From up front his words barely carried to the middle of the auditorium: 'Thosewhocomeafterus – Andinthishour – whenthetravellerreturns – butthistimethehomeland – andletusnever – pureofheart – asIsaidbefore – pureofheart – andifanyonedisagreeslet – andinthishour – keepclean – toconcludewiththewordsofSchiller – ifyourlifeyoudonotstake – thelaurelneverwillyoutake – Andnow backtowork!'

Dismissed, we formed two clusters at the narrow exits. I pushed in behind Mahlke. He was sweating and his sugar-water hair stood up in sticky blades around his ravaged parting. Never, not even in gym, had I seen Mahlke perspire. The stench of three hundred schoolboys stuck like corks in the exits. Beads of sweat stood out on Mahlke's flushed anxiety cords, those two bundles of sinew running from the seventh vertebra of his neck to the base of his jutting occiput. In the colonnade outside the folding doors, amid the hubbub of the small boys, who had resumed their perpetual game of tag, I caught up with him. I questioned him head on: 'Well, what do you say?'

Mahlke stared straight ahead. I tried not to look at his neck. Between two columns stood a plaster bust of Lessing: but Mahlke's neck won out. Calmly and mournfully as though speaking on his aunt's chronic ailments, his voice said: 'Now they need a bag of forty if they want the medal. At the beginning and after they were through in France and in the North, it only took twenty – if it keeps on like this . . . '

I suppose the lieutenant's talk didn't agree with you. Or you wouldn't have resorted to such cheap compensations. In those days luminous buttons and round, oval, or open-work plaques were on display in the windows of stationery and dry-goods stores. They glowed milky-green in the darkness, some disclosing the contours of a fish, others of a flying gull. These little plaques were purchased mostly by elderly gentlemen and fragile old ladies, who wore them on their coat collars for fear of collisions in the black-out; there were also walking sticks with luminous stripes.

You were not afraid of the blackout, and yet you fastened five or six plaques, a luminous school of fish, a flock of gliding gulls, several bouquets of phosphorescent flowers, first on the lapels of your coat, then on your muffler; you had your aunt sew half a dozen luminous buttons from top to bottom of your coat; you turned yourself into a clown. In the winter twilight, through slanting snowflakes or well-nigh uniform darkness, I saw you, I still see you and always will, striding towards me down Bärenweg, enumerable from top to bottom and back, with one two three four five six coat buttons glowing mouldy-green: a pathetic sort of ghost, capable at most of scaring children and grandmothers – trying to distract attention from an affliction which no one could have seen in the pitch darkness. But you said to yourself no doubt: no blackness can engulf this overdeveloped fruit; everyone sees, suspects, feels it, wants to grab hold of it, for it juts out ready to be grabbed; if only this winter were over, so I could dive again and be under water.

Chapter Six

But when the summer came with strawberries, special communiqués and bathing weather, Mahlke didn't want to swim. On the first of June we swam out to the barge for the first time. We weren't really in the mood. We were annoyed at the Third Form boys who swam with us and ahead of us, who sat on the bridge in swarms, dived, and brought up the last hinge that could be unscrewed. 'Let me come with you, I can swim now,' Mahlke had once pleaded. And now it was Schilling, Winter and myself who pestered him: 'Oh, come along. It's no fun without you. We can sun ourselves on the barge. Maybe you'll find something interesting down below.'

Reluctantly, after waving us away several times, Mahlke stepped into the tepid soup between the beach and the first sand bank. He swam without his screwdriver, stayed between us, two arms' lengths behind Hotten Sonntag, and for the first time I saw him swim calmly, without excitement or splashing. On the bridge he sat huddled in the shadow of the pilot house and no one could persuade him to dive. He didn't even turn his neck when the Third Formers vanished into the fo'c'sle and came up with trinkets. Yet Mahlke could have taught them a thing or two. Some of them even asked him for pointers – but he scarcely answered. The whole time he looked out through puckered eyes over the open sea in the direction of the harbour mouth buoy, but neither inbound freighters, nor outbound cutters, nor a formation of torpedo boats could divert him. Maybe the submarines got a slight rise out of him. Sometimes, far out at sea, the periscope of a sub-merged U-boat could be seen cutting a distinct stripe of foam. The 750-ton vessels, built in series at the Schichau shipyards, were given trial runs in the Gulf or behind Hela;

52

surfacing in the deep channel, they put in toward the harbour and dispelled our boredom. Looked good as they rose to the surface, periscope first. The moment the conning tower emerged, it spat out one or two figures. In dull-white streams the water receded from the gun, ran off the bow and then the stern. Men scrambled out of the hatches, we shouted and waved – I'm not sure whether they answered us, though I still see the motion of waving in every detail and can still feel it in my shoulders. Whether or not they waved back, the surfacing of a submarine strikes the heart, still does – but Mahlke never waved.

... and once – it was the end of June, summer vacation hadn't started yet and the lieutenant commander hadn't yet delivered his lecture in our school auditorium – Mahlke left his place in the shade because a Third Former had gone down into the fo'c'sle of the mine sweeper and hadn't come up. Mahlke went down the hatch and brought the kid up. He had wedged himself in amidships, but he hadn't got as far as the engine room. Mahlke found him under the deck between pipes and bundles of cable. For two hours Schilling and Hotten Sonntag took turns working on the kid according to Mahlke's directions. Gradually, the colour came back into his face, but when we swam ashore we had to tow him.

Then next day Mahlke was diving again with his usual enthusiasm, but without a screwdriver. He swam across at his usual speed, leaving us all behind; he had already been under once when we climbed up on the bridge.

The preceding winter's ice and February storms had carried away the last bit of rail, both gun mounts, and the top of the pilot house. Only the encrusted gull droppings had come through in good shape and, if anything, had multiplied. Mahlke brought up nothing and didn't answer the questions we kept thinking up. But late in the afternoon, after he had been down ten or twelve times and we were starting to limber up for the swim back, he went down and didn't come up. We were all of us out of our minds.

When I speak of a five-minute intermission, it doesn't mean a thing; but after five minutes as long as years, that we occupied with swallowing until our tongues lay thick and dry in dry hollows, we dived down into the barge one by one: in the fo'c'sle there was nothing but a few herring fry. Behind Hotten Sonntag I ventured through the bulkhead for the first time, and looked superficially about the former officers' mess. Then I had to come up, shot out of the hatch just before I would have burst, went down again, shoved my way twice more through the bulkhead, and didn't give up until a good half hour later. Seven or eight of us lay flat on the bridge, panting. The gulls circled closer and closer; must have noticed something.

Luckily there were no Third Formers on the barge. We were all silent or all talking at once. The gulls flew off to one side and came back again. We cooked up stories for the lifeguard, for Mahlke's mother and aunt, and for Klohse, because there was sure to be an investigation at school. Because I was Mahlke's neighbour, they saddled me with the visit to his mother on Osterzeile. Schilling was to tell our story to the lifeguard and in school.

'If they don't find him, we'll have to swim out here with a wreath and have a ceremony.'

'We'll chip in. We'll each contribute at least fifty pfennigs.'

'We can throw him overboard from here, or maybe just lower him into the fo'c'sle.'

'We'll have to sing something,' said Kupka. But the hollow tinkling laughter that followed this suggestion did not originate with any of us: it came from inside the bridge. We all gaped at some unknown point, waiting for

54

the laughter to start up again, but when it did, it was a perfectly normal kind of laughter, had lost its hollowness and came from the fo'c'sle. The waters parting at his watershed, Mahlke pushed out of the hatch, breathing scarcely harder than usual and rubbed the fresh sunburn on his neck and shoulders. His bleating was more good-natured than scornful. 'Well,' he said, 'have you got that funeral oration ready?'

Before we swam to shore, Mahlke went down again. Winter was having an attack of the weeping jitters and we were trying to pacify him. Fifteen minutes later Winter was still bawling, and Mahlke was back on the bridge, wearing a set of radio operator's ear phones which from the outside at least looked undamaged, almost new; for amidships Mahlke had found the way into a room that was situated inside the command bridge, above the surface of the water; the former radio shack. The place was bone dry, he said, though somewhat clammy. After consider-able stalling he admitted that he had discovered the entrance while disentangling the young Third Former from the pipes and cables. 'I've camouflaged it. Nobody'll ever find it. But it was lots of work. It's my private property now, in case you have any doubts. Cosy little spot. Good place to hide if things get hot. Lots of apparatus, trans-mitter and so on. Might try to put in working order one of these days.'

But that was beyond Mahlke's abilities and I doubt if he ever tried. Or if he did tinker some without letting on, I'm sure his efforts were unsuccessful. He was very handy and knew all there was to know about making ship models, but he was hardly a radio technician. Besides, if Mahlke had ever got the transmitter working and started broadcasting witty sayings, the Navy or the harbour police would have picked us up.

In actual fact, he removed all the apparatus from the cabin and gave it to Kupka, Esch, and the Third Formers;

all he kept for himself was the ear phones. He wore them a whole week, and it was only when he began systematically to refurnish the radio shack that he threw them overboard.

The first thing he moved in was books – I don't remember exactly what they were. My guess is that they included *Tsuschima, The Story of a Naval Battle*, a volume or two of Dwinger, and some religious stuff. He wrapped them first in old woollen blankets, then in oil cloth, and caulked the seams with pitch or tar or wax. The bundle was carried out to the barge on a driftwood raft which he, with occasional help from us, towed behind him as he swam. He claimed that the books and blankets had reached their destination almost dry. The next shipment consisted of candles, spirit stove, fuel, an aluminium pot, tea, oat flakes and dehydrated vegetables. Often he was gone for as much as an hour; we would begin to pound frantically, but he never answered. Of course we admired him. But Mahlke ignored our admiration and grew more and more monosyllabic; in the end he wouldn't even let us help him with his moving. However, it was in our presence that he rolled up the colour print of the Sistine Madonna, known to me from his room on Osterzeile, and stuffed it inside a hollow curtain rod, packing the open ends with modelling clay. Madonna and curtain rod were towed to the barge and manoeuvred into the cabin. At last I knew why he was knocking himself out, for whom he was furnishing the former radio shack.

My guess is that the print was damaged in diving, or perhaps that the moisture in the airless cabin (it had no port holes or communication with the ventilators, which were all flooded in the first place) did not agree with it, for a few days later Mahlke was wearing something on his neck again, appended to a black shoelace: not a screwdriver, but the bronze medallion with the so-called Black Madonna of Czestochowa in low relief. Our eyebrows shot up knowingly; ha-ha, we thought, there's the Madonna routine again. Before we had time to settle ourselves on the bridge, Mahlke disappeared down the forward hatch. He was back again in no more than fifteen minutes, without shoelace and medallion, and he seemed pleased as he resumed his place behind the pilot house.

He was whistling. That was the first time I heard Mahlke whistle. Of course he wasn't whistling for the first time, but it was the first time I noticed his whistling, which is tantamount to saying that he was really pursing his lips for the first time. I alone – being the only other Catholic on the barge – knew what the whistling was about: he whistled one hymn to the Virgin after another. Leaning on a vestige of the rail, he began with aggressive good humour to beat time on the rickety side of the bridge with his dangling feet; then over the muffled din, he reeled off the whole Pentecost sequence '*Veni, Sancte Spiritus*' and after that – I had been expecting it – the sequence for the Friday before Palm Sunday. All ten stanzas of the *Stabat Mater dolorosa* including *Paradisi Gloria* and *Amen*, were rattled off without a hitch. I myself, who had once been Father Gusewski's most devoted altar boy but whose attendance had become very irregular of late, could barely have recollected the first lines.

Mahlke, however, served Latin to the gulls with the utmost ease, and the others, Schilling, Kupka, Esch, Hotten Sonntag and whoever else was there, listened eagerly with a 'Boyohboy' and 'Ittakesyourbreathaway'. They even asked Mahlke to repeat the *Stabat Mater*, though nothing could have been more remote from their interests than Latin and liturgical texts.

Still, I don't think you were planning to turn the radio shack into a chapel for the Virgin. Most of the rubbish that found its way there had nothing to do with her. Though I never inspected your hideout – we simply couldn't make it – I see it as a miniature edition of your attic room on Osterzeile. Only the geraniums and cacti which your aunt, often against your will, lodged on the window sill and the four-storey cactus racks, had no counterpart in the former radio shack; otherwise your moving was a perfect job.

After the books and cooking utensils, Mahlke's ship models, the dispatch boat *Cricket* and the torpedo boat of the *Wolff* class, scale 1:1250, were moved below decks. Ink, several pens, a ruler, a school compass, his butterfly collection and the stuffed snowy owl were also obliged to take the dive. I presume that Mahlke's furnishings gradually began to look pretty sick in this room where water vapour could do nothing but condense. Especially the butterflies in their glassed-over cigar boxes, accustomed as they were to dry attic air, must have suffered from the dampness.

But what we admired most about this game of removal man, which went on for days, was precisely its absurdity and deliberate destructiveness. And the zeal with which Joachim Mahlke gradually returned to the former Polish mine sweeper so many of the objects which he had painstakingly removed two summers before – good old Pilsudski, the plates with the instructions for operating this or that machine, and so on – enabled us, despite the irritating Third Formers, to spend an entertaining, I might even say exciting summer on that barge for which the war had lasted only four weeks.

To give you an example of our pleasures: Mahlke offered us music. You will remember that in the summer of 1940, after he had swum out to the barge with us perhaps six or seven times, he had slowly and painstakingly salvaged a gramophone from the fo'c'sle or the officer's mess, that he had taken it home, repaired it and put on a new turntable covered with felt. This same gramophone, along with ten or a dozen records, was one of the last items to find its way back again. The moving took two days, during which time he couldn't resist the temptation to wear the crank round his neck, suspended from his trusty shoelace.

Gramophone and records must have come through the trip through the flooded fo'c'sle and the bulkhead in good shape, for that same afternoon he surprised us with music, a hollow tinkling whose source seemed to shift eerily about but was always somewhere inside the barge. I shouldn't be surprised if it shook loose the rivets and sheathing. Though the sun was far down in the sky, we were still getting some of it on the bridge, but even so that sound gave us gooseflesh. Of course we would shout: 'Stop it. No. Go on! Play another!' I remember a well-known *Ave Maria*, as long-lasting as a wad of chewing gum, which smoothed the choppy sea; he just couldn't manage without the Virgin.

There were also arias, overtures, and suchlike – have I told you that Mahlke was gone on serious music? From the inside out Mahlke regaled us with something passionate from Tosca, something enchanted from Humperdinck, and part of a symphony beginning with dadada daaah, known to us from popular concerts.

Schilling and Kupka shouted for something hot, but that he didn't have. It was Zarah who produced the most startling effects. Her underwater voice laid us out flat on the rust and bumpy gull droppings. I don't remember what she sang in that first record. It was always the same Zarah. In one, though, she sang something from an opera with which we had been familiarized by a film called *Homeland*. 'AlasIhavelosther,' she moaned. 'Thewind sangmeasong,' she sighed. 'Onedayamiraclewillhappen,' she prophesied. She could sound organ tones and conjure the elements, or she could dispense moments of languor and tenderness. Winter hardly bothered to stifle his sobs and in general our eyelashes were kept pretty busy.

And over it all the gulls. They were always getting frantic over nothing, but when Zarah revolved on the turntable down below, they went completely out of their heads. Their glass-cutting screams, emanating no doubt from the souls of departed tenors, rose high over the much imitated and yet inimitable, dungeon-deep plaint of this tear-jerking film star gifted with a voice, who in the war years earned an immense popularity on every front including the home front.

Mahlke treated us several times to this concert until the records were so worn that nothing emerged but a tortured gurgling and scratching. To this day no music has given me greater pleasure, though I seldom miss a concert at Robert Schumann Hall and whenever I am in funds purchase long-playing records ranging from Monteverdi to Bartók. Silent and insatiable, we huddled over the gramophone, which we called the Ventriloquist. We had run out of praises. Of course we admired Mahlke; but in the eerie din our admiration shifted into its opposite, and we thought him so repulsive we couldn't look, at him. Then, as a low-lying freighter hove into view we felt moderately sorry for him. We were also afraid of Mahlke; he bullied us. And I was ashamed to be seen in the street with him. And I was proud when Hotten Sonntag's sister or the little Pokriefke girl met the two of us together outside the Art Cinema or on Heeresanger. You were our theme song. We would lay bets: 'What's he going to do now? I bet you he's got a sore throat again. I'm taking all bets: Some day he's going to hang himself, or he'll get to be something real big, or invent something terrific.'

And Schilling said to Hotten Sonntag: 'Tell me the honest truth; if your sister went out with Mahlke, to the pictures and all, tell me the honest truth; what would you do?'

Chapter Seven

The appearance of the lieutenant commander and much decorated U-boat captain in the auditorium of our school put an end to the concerts from within the former Polish mine sweeper *Rybitwa*. Even if he had not turned up, the records and the gramophone couldn't have held out for more than another three or four days. But he did turn up, and without having to pay a visit to our barge, he turned off the underwater music and gave all our conversations about Mahlke a new, though not fundamentally new, turn.

The lieutenant commander must have graduated in about '34. It was said that before volunteering for the Navy he had studied some at the university: theology and German literature. I can't help it, I am obliged to call his eyes fiery. His hair was thick and kinky, maybe wiry would be the word, and there was something of the old Roman about his head. No submariner's beard, but aggressive eyebrows that suggested an overhanging roof. His forehead was that of a philosopher-saint, hence no horizontal wrinkles, but two vertical lines, beginning at the bridge of the nose and rising in search of God. The light played on the uppermost point of the bold vault. Nose small and sharp. The mouth he opened for us was a delicately curved orator's mouth. The auditorium was overcrowded with people and morning sun. We were forced to huddle in the window niches. Whose idea had it been to invite the two upper classes of the Gudrun School? The girls occupied the front rows of benches; they should have worn brassières, but didn't.

When the proctor called us to the lecture, Mahlke hadn't wanted to attend. Flairing some possible gain in prestige for myself, I took him by the sleeve. Beside me, in the window niche – behind us the windowpanes and the motionless chestnut trees in the recreation yard – Mahlke began to tremble before the lieutenant commander had even opened his mouth. Mahlke's hands clutched Mahlke's knees, but the trembling continued. The teachers, including two lady teachers from the Gudrun School, occupied a semicircle of oak chairs with high backs and leather cushions, which the proctor had set up with remarkable precision. Dr Moeller clapped his hands, and little by little the audience quieted down for Dr Klohse, our principal. Behind the twin braids and pony tails of the upper-class girls sat Fourth Formers with pocket-knives; braids were quickly shifted from back to front. Only the pony tails remained within reach of the Fourth Formers and their knives. This time there was an introduction. Klohse spoke of all those who are out there fighting for us, on land, on the sea, and in the air, spoke at length and with little inflection of himself and the students at Langemarck, and on the Isle of Osel fell Walter Flex, quotation: Maturebutpure: the manly virtues. Then some Fichte or Arndt. Quotation: On youaloneandwhatyoudo. Recollection of an excellent paper on Fichte or Arndt that the lieutenant commander had written in Second Form: 'One of us, from our midst, a product of our school and its spirit, and in this spirit let us . . . '

Need I say how zealously notes were passed back and forth between us in the window niches and the girls from the Upper Second. Of course the Fourth Formers mixed in a few obscenities of their own. I wrote a note saying Godknowswhat either to Vera Plötz or to Hildchen Matull, but got no answer from either. Mahlke's hands were still clutching Mahlke's knees. The trembling died down. The lieutenant commander on the platform sat slightly crushed between old Dr Brunies who as usual was calmly sucking boiled sweets and Dr Stachnitz, our Latin teacher. As the introduction droned to an end, as our notes passed back and forth, as the Fourth Formers with pocket-knives, as the eyes of the Führer's photograph met those of the oil-painted Baron von Conradi, as the morning sun slipped out of the auditorium, the lieutenant commander moistened his delicately curved orator's mouth and stared morosely at the audience, making a heroic effort to exclude the girl students from his field of vision. Cap perched with dignity on his parallel knees. Under the cap his gloves. Dress uniform. The hardware on his neck plainly discernible against an inconceivably white shirt. Sudden movement of his head, half followed by his decoration, towards the lateral windows: Mahlke trembled, feeling no doubt that he had been recognized, but he hadn't. Through the window in whose niche we huddled the U-boat captain gazed at dusty, motionless chestnut trees; what I thought then or think now, what can he be thinking, what can Mahlke be thinking, or Klohse while speaking, or Brunies while sucking, or Vera Plötz while your note, or Hildchen Matull, what can he he he be thinking, Mahlke or the fellow with the orator's mouth? For it would have been illuminating to know what a U-boat captain thinks while obliged to listen, while his gaze roams free without cross-wires and dancing horizon, until Joachim Mahlke feels singled out; but actually he was staring over schoolboys' heads, through double windowpanes at the dry greenness of the poker-faced trees in the recreation yard, giving his orator's mouth one last moistening with his bright-red tongue, for Klohse was trying, with words on peppermint breath, to send a last sentence out past the middle of the auditorium: 'And today it beseems us in the homeland to give our full attention to what you sons of our nation have to report from the front, from every front.'

The orator's mouth had deceived us. The lieutenant

commander started out with a very colourless survey such as one might have found in any naval manual: The function of the submarine. German submarines in the First World War: Weddigen and the U9, submarine plays decisive role in Dardanelles campaign, sinking a total of thirteen million gross register tons. Our first 250-ton subs, electric when submerged, diesel on the surface, the name of Prien was dropped, Prien and the U47, and Lieutenant Commander Prien sent the *Royal Oak* to the bottom – hell, we knew all that – as well as the *Repulse*, and Schuhart sank the *Courageous*, and so on and so on. And then all the old saws: 'The crew is a body of men who have sworn to stand together in life and death, far from home, terrible nervous strain, you can imagine, living in a sardine tin in the middle of the Atlantic or the Arctic, cramped humid hot, men obliged to sleep on spare torpedoes, nothing stirring for days on end, empty horizon, then suddenly a convoy, heavily guarded, everything has to go like clockwork, not an unnecessary syllable; when we bagged our first tanker, the *Arndale*, 17,200 tons, with two fish amidships, believe it or not, I thought of you, my dear Dr Stachnitz, and began to recite out loud, without turning off the intercom, *qui quae quod, cuius cuius cuius* . . . until our exec called back. Good work, skipper, you may take the rest of the day off. But a submarine mission isn't all shooting and tube one fire and tube two fire; for days on end it's the same monotonous sea, the rolling and pounding of the boat, and overhead the sky, a sky to make your head reel, I tell you, and sunsets . . . '

Although the lieutenant commander with the hardware on his neck had sunk 250,000 gross register tons, a light cruiser of the *Despatch* class and a heavy destroyer of the *Tribal* class, the details of his exploits took up much less space in his talk than verbose descriptions of nature. No metaphor was too daring. For instance: ' . . . swaying like a train of priceless, dazzlingly white lace, the foaming wake follows the boat which, swathed like a bride in festive veils of spray, strides onward to the marriage of death.'

The tittering wasn't limited to the pigtail contingent; but in the ensuing metaphor the bride was obliterated: 'A submarine is like a whale with a hump, but what of its bow wave? It is like the twirling, many times twirled moustaches of a hussar.'

The lieutenant commander also had a way of intoning dry technical terms as if they had been dark words of legend. Probably his lecture was addressed more to Papa Brunies, his former German teacher, known as a lover of Eichendorff, than to us. Klohse had mentioned the eloquence of his school themes and perhaps he wished to show that his tongue had lost none of its cunning. Such words as 'bilge pump' or 'helmsman' were uttered in a mysterious whisper. He must have thought he was offering us a revelation when he said 'master compass' or 'repeater compass'. Good Lord, we had known all this stuff for years. He saw himself as the kindly grandmother telling fairy tales. The voice in which he spoke of a dog-watch or a water-tight door or even something as commonplace as a 'choppy cross sea'! It was like listening to dear old Andersen or the Brothers Grimm telling a spooky tale about 'Asdic-impulses.'

When he started brushing in sunsets, it was really embarrassing: 'And before the Atlantic night descends on us like a flock of ravens transformed by enchantment into a black shroud, the sky takes on colours we never see at home. An orange flares up, fleshy and unnatural, then airy and weightless, bejewelled at the edges as in the paintings of old masters; and in between, feathery clouds; and oh what a strange light over the rolling full-blooded sea!'

Standing there with his sugar candy on his neck, he

sounded the colour organ, rising to a roar, descending to a whisper, from watery-blue to cold-glazed lemon yellow to brownish-purple. Poppies blazed in the sky, and in their midst clouds, first silver, then suffused with red: 'So must it be,' these were his actual words, 'when birds and angels bleed to death.' And suddenly from out of this sky, so daringly described, from out of bucolic little clouds, he conjured up a flying-boat of the *Sunderland* type. It came buzzing toward his U-boat but accomplished nothing. Then with the same orator's mouth but without metaphors, he opened the second part of his lecture. Chopped, dry, matter-of-fact: 'I'm sitting in the periscope seat. Just scored a hit. Probably a refrigerator ship. Sinks stern first. We take the boat down at one one zero. Destroyer comes in on one seven zero. We come left ten degrees. New course: one two zero, steady on one two zero. Propeller sounds fade, increase, come in at one eight zero, ash cans: six ... seven ... eight ... eleven: lights go out; pitch darkness, then the emergency lighting comes on, and one after another the stations report all clear. Destroyer has stopped. Last bearing one six zero, we come left ten degrees. New course four five ... '

Unfortunately this really exciting fillet was followed by more prose poems: 'The Atlantic winter' or 'Phosphorescence in the Mediterranean', and a genre painting: 'Christmas on a submarine', with the inevitable broom transformed into a Christmas tree. In conclusion he rose to mythical heights: the homecoming after a successful mission, Ulysses, and at long last: 'The first sea-gulls tell us that the port is near.'

I don't know whether Dr Klohse ended the session with the familiar words: 'And now back to work', or whether we sang 'Welovethestorms'. I seem, rather, to recall muffled but respectful applause, disorganized movements of getting up, begun by girls and pigtails. When I turned around toward Mahlke, he was gone; I saw his hair with the parting in the middle bob up several times by the righthand exit, but one of my legs had fallen asleep during the lecture and for a few moments I was unable to jump from the window niche to the waxed floor.

It wasn't until I reached the dressing room by the gymnasium that I ran into Mahlke; but I could think of nothing to start a conversation with. While we were still changing, rumours were heard and soon confirmed. We were being honoured: the lieutenant commander had asked Mallenbrandt, his former gym teacher, for leave to participate in the good old gym class, though he was out of shape. In the course of the two hours which as usual on Saturday closed the school day, he showed us what he could do. In the second hour, we were joined by the First Class.

Squat, well built, with a luxuriant growth of black hair on his chest. From Mallenbrandt he had borrowed the traditional red gym pants, the white shirt with the red stripe at chest level, and the black C embedded in the stripe. A cluster of students formed round him while he was dressing. Lots of questions:' ... may I look at it close up? How long does it take? And what if? But a friend of my brother's in the mosquito boats says ... ' He answered patiently. Sometimes he laughed for no reason but contagiously. The dressing room whinnied; and the only reason why Mahlke caught my attention just then was that he didn't join in the laughter; he was busy folding and hanging up his clothes.

The trill of Mallenbrandt's whistle called us to the gymnasium, where we gathered around the horizontal bar. The lieutenant commander, discreetly seconded by Mallenbrandt, directed the class. Which meant that we were not kept very busy, because he was determined to perform for us, among other things the giant swing ending in a leg squat. Aside from Hotten Sonntag only Mahlke could compete, but so execrable were his swing and squat –

his knees were bent and he was all tensed up – that none of us could bear to watch him. When the lieutenant commander began to lead us in a series of free and carefully graduated ground exercises, Mahlke's Adam's apple was still dancing about like a stuck pig. In the vault over seven men, he landed askew on the mat and apparently turned his ankle. After that he sat on a ladder off to one side and must have slipped away when the First joined us at the beginning of the second hour. However, he was back again for the basketball game against the First, he even made three or four baskets, but we lost just the same.

Our neo-Gothic gymnasium preserved its air of solemnity just as St Mary's Chapel in Neuschottland, regardless of all the painted plaster and ecclesiastical trappings Father Gusewski could assemble in the bright gymnastic light of its broad window fronts, never lost the feel of the modern gymnasium it had formerly been. While there clarity prevailed over all mysteries, we trained our muscles in a mysterious twilight: our gymnasium had ogival windows, their panes broken up by rosettes and flamboyant tracery. In the glaring light of St Mary's Chapel, offering, trans-substantiation and communion were disenchanted motions that might have been performed in a factory; instead of wafers, one might just as well have handed out hammers, saws or window frames, or for that matter gymnastic apparatus, bats and relay sticks as in former days. While in the mystical light of our gymnasium the simple act of choosing the two basketball teams, whose ten minutes of play was to wind up the session, seemed solemnly moving like an ordination or confirmation ceremony; and when the chosen ones stepped aside into the dim background, it was with the humility of those performing a sacred rite. Especially on bright mornings, when a few rays of sun found their way through the foliage in the yard and the ogival windows, the oblique beams, falling on the moving figures of athletes performing on the trapeze or rings, produced strange, romantic effects. If I concentrate, I can still see the squat little lieutenant commander in altar-boy-red gym pants, executing airy, fluid movements on the flying trapeze, I can see his flawlessly pointed feet – he performed bare-foot – diving into a golden sunbeam, and I can see his hands – for all at once he was hanging by his knees – reach out for a shaft of agitated golden dust. Yes, our gymnasium was marvellously old-fashioned; why, even the dressing room obtained its light through ogival windows; that was why we called it the Sacristy.

Mallenbrandt blew his whistle; after the basketball game both classes had to line up and sing: 'Tothemountainswegointheearlydewfallera'; then we were dismissed. In the dressing room there was again a huddle round the lieutenant commander. Only the First hung back a little. After carefully washing his hands and armpits over the one and only wash basin – there were no showers – the lieutenant commander put on his underwear and stripped off his borrowed gym togs so deftly that we didn't see a thing. Meanwhile he was subjected to more questions which he answered with a good-natured, not too condescending laughter. Then, between two questions, his good humour left him. His hands groped uncertainly. Covertly at first, then openly, he was looking for something. He even looked under the bench. 'Just a minute, boys, I'll be back on deck in a second,' and in navy-blue shorts, white shirt, socks but no shoes, he picked his way through students, benches, and zoo smell: Pavilion for Small Carnivores. His collar stood open and raised, ready to receive his tie and the ribbon bearing the decoration whose name I dare not utter. On the door of Mallenbrandt's office hung the weekly gymnasium schedule. The lieutenant commander knocked and went right in.

Who didn't think of Mahlke as I did? I'm not sure I thought of him right away, I should have, but the one thing I am sure of is that I didn't sing out: 'Hey, where's Mahlke?' Nor did Schilling nor Hotten Sonntag, nor Winter Kupka Esch. Nobody sang out; instead we all ganged up on sickly little Buschmann, a poor devil who had come into the world with a grin that he couldn't wipe off his face even after it had been slapped a dozen times.

The half-dressed lieutenant commander came back with Mallenbrandt in a terry-cloth bathrobe. 'Whowasit?' Mallenbrandt roared. 'Lethimstepforward!' And we sacrificed Buschmann to his wrath. I too shouted Buschmann; I even succeeded in telling myself as though I really believed it: Yes, it must have been Buschmann, who else could it be?

But while Mallenbrandt, the lieutenant commander and the upper-class monitor were flinging questions at Buschmann all together, I began to have pins and needles, superficially at first, on the back of my neck. The sensation grew stronger when Buschmann got his first slap, when he was slapped because even under questioning he couldn't get the grin off his face. While my eyes and ears waited for a clear confession from Buschmann, the certainty crawled upward from the back of my neck: Say, I wonder if it wasn't a certain So-and-so!

My confidence seeped away; no, the grinning Buschmann was not going to confess; even Mallenbrandt must have suspected as much or he would not have been so liberal with his slaps. He had stopped talking about the missing object and only roared between one slap and the next: 'Wipe that grin off your face. Stop it, I say. I'll teach you to grin.'

I may say, in passing, that Mallenbrandt did not achieve his aim. I don't know whether Buschmann is still in existence; but if there should be a dentist, veterinary surgeon, or physician by the name of Buschmann – Heini Buschmann was planning to study medicine – it is certainly a grinning Dr Buschmann; for that kind of thing is not so easily got rid of, it is long-lived, survives wars and currency reforms, and even then, in the presence of a lieutenant commander with an empty collar, waiting for an investigation to produce results, it proved superior to the blows of Dr Mallenbrandt, our form master.

Discreetly, though all eyes were on Buschmann, I looked for Mahlke, but there was no need to search; I could tell by a feel in my neck where he was inwardly singing his hymn to the Virgin. Fully dressed, not far away but removed from the crowd, he was buttoning the top button of a shirt which to judge by the cut and stripes must have been still another hand-me-down from his father. He was having trouble getting his distinguishing mark in under the button.

Apart from his struggles with his shirt button and the accompanying efforts of his jaw muscles, he gave an impression of calm. When he realized that the button wouldn't close over his Adam's apple, he reached into the breast pocket of his coat that was still hanging up and produced a rumpled necktie. No one in our class wore a tie. In the upper classes there were a few fops who affected ridiculous bow ties. Two hours before, while the lieutenant was still regaling the auditorium about the beauties of nature, he had worn his shirt collar open; but already the tie was in his breast pocket, awaiting the great occasion.

This was Mahlke's maiden voyage as a necktie wearer. There was only one mirror in the dressing room and even so it was covered with spots. Standing before it, but only for the sake of form, for he didn't step close enough to see anything much, he tied on his rag – it had bright polka dots and was in very bad taste, I am convinced today – turned down his collar, and gave the enormous knot one last tug. Then he spoke up, not in a very loud voice but with sufficient emphasis that his words could be distinguished from the sounds of the investigation that was still in progress and the slaps which Mallenbrandt, over the lieutenant commander's objections, was still tirelessly meting out. 'I'm willing to bet,' Mahlke said, 'that Buschmann didn't do it. But has anybody searched his clothing?'

Though he had spoken to the mirror, Mahlke found ready listeners. His necktie, his new act, was noticed only later, and then not very much. Mallenbrandt personally searched Buschmann's clothes and soon found reason to strike another blow at the grin; in both coat pockets he found several opened packages of condoms, with which Buschmann carried on a retail trade in the upper classes, his father was a druggist. Otherwise Mallenbrandt found nothing, and the lieutenant commander cheerfully gave up, knotted his officer's tie, turned his collar down, and tapping at the spot which had previously been so eminently decorated, suggested to Mallenbrandt that there was no need to take the incident too seriously: 'It's easily replaced. It's not the end of the world. Just a silly boyish prank.'

But Mallenbrandt had the doors of the gymnasium and dressing room locked and with the help of two First Formers searched our pockets as well as every corner of the room that might have been used as a hiding place. At first the lieutenant commander was amused and even helped, but after a while he grew impatient and did something that no one had ever dared to do in our dressing room: he began to chain smoke, stamping out the butts on the linoleum floor. His mood soured visibly after Mallenbrandt had silently pushed up a spittoon which for years had been gathering dust beside the wash bowl and had already been searched as a possible hiding place.

The lieutenant commander blushed like a schoolboy, tore the cigarette he had just begun from his delicately curved orator's mouth, and stopped smoking. At first he just stood there with his arms folded; then he began to look nervously at the time, demonstrating his impatience by the sharp left hook with which he shook his wrist watch out of his sleeve.

He took his leave by the door with gloved fingers, giving it to be understood that he could not approve of the way this investigation was being handled, that he would put the whole irritating business into the hands of the principal, for he had no intention of letting his leave be spoiled by a bunch of ill-behaved brats.

Mallenbrandt tossed the key to one of the First Formers who created an embarrassing pause by his clumsiness in unlocking the dressing room door.

Chapter Eight

The investigation dragged on, ruining our Saturday afternoon and bringing no results. I remember few details and those are hardly worth talking about, for I had to keep an eye on Mahlke and his necktie, whose knot he periodically tried to push up higher; but for Mahlke's purposes a hook would have been needed. No, you were beyond help.

But what of the lieutenant commander? The question seems hardly worth asking, but it can be answered in few words. He was not present at the afternoon investigation, and it may well have been true, as unconfirmed rumours had it, that he spent the afternoon with his fiancée, looking through the city's three or four medal shops. Somebody in our class claimed to have seen him on Sunday at the Four Seasons Café, sitting with his fiancée and her parents, and allegedly nothing was missing between his collarbones: the visitors to the café may have noticed with a certain awe who was sitting there in their midst, trying his well-mannered best to cut the recalcitrant cake of the third war year with a fork.

I didn't go to the café that Sunday. I had promised

Father Gusewski to serve as his altar boy at early Mass. Shortly after seven Mahlke came in with his bright necktie and was unable, despite the aid of the usual five little old women, to dispel the emptiness of the former gymnasium. He received communion as usual on the outer left. The previous evening, immediately after the investigation at school, he must have come to St Mary's Chapel and confessed; or perhaps, for one reason or another, you whispered into Father Wiehnke's ear at the Church of the Sacred Heart.

Gusewski kept me, inquired after my brother who was fighting in Russia, or maybe he had stopped fighting, for there had been no news of him for several weeks. Once again I had ironed and starched all the altar covers and the alb, and it is perfectly possible that he gave me a roll or two of raspberry drops; what I know for sure is that Mahlke was gone when I left the sacristy. He must have been one tram ahead of me. On Max-Halbe-Platz I boarded the trailer-car of a No. 9 tram. Schilling jumped on at Magdeburger-Strasse after the tram had gathered considerable speed. We spoke of something entirely different. Maybe I offered him some of Father Gusewski's raspberry drops. Between Saspe Manor and Saspe Cemetery, we overtook Hotten Sonntag. He was riding a lady's bicycle and carrying the little Pokriefke girl astraddle on the baggage rack. The spindly little thing's thighs were still as smooth as frog's legs, but she was no longer flat all over. The wind showed that her hair had grown longer.

We had to wait at the Saspe siding for the tram coming from the opposite direction, and Hotten Sonntag and Tulla passed us. At the Brösen stop the two of them were waiting. The bicycle was leaning against a waste paper basket provided by the beach administration. They were playing brother and sister, standing there with their little fingers linked. Tulla's dress was blue, blue washing blue,

74

and in every way too short too tight too blue. Hotten Sonntag was carrying the bundle of bathrobes, etc. We managed to exchange a few silent glances, and to catch each other's meaning. At length words fell from the supercharged silence: 'Of course it was Mahlke, who else could it have been? What a chap!'

Tulla wanted details, squirmed up to us, and wheedled with a pointed forefinger. But neither of us called the object by name. She got no more out of us than a terse 'WhoelsebutMahlke' and an 'Itsasclearasday'. But Schilling, no, it was I, dreamed up a new title. Into the gap between Hotten Sonntag's head and Tulla's head I inserted the words: 'The Great Mahlke. The Great Mahlke did it, only the Great Mahlke can do such things.'

And the title stuck. All previous attempts to fasten nicknames to Mahlke had been shortlived. I remember 'Soup Chicken'; and when he stood aloof, we had called him 'Swallower' or 'The Swallower'. But the first title to prove viable was my spontaneous cry: 'The Great Mahlke!' And in these papers I shall speak now and then of 'The Great Mahlke.'

At the cashier's window we got rid of Tulla. She disappeared into the ladies' cabins, stretching her dress with her shoulder-blades. Before the veranda-like structure in front of the men's bath house lay the sea, pale and shaded by fair-weather clouds, blowing across the sky in dispersed order. Water: 65. Without having to search, the three of us caught sight, behind the second sandbank, of somebody swimming frantically on his back, splashing and foaming as he headed for the superstructure of the mine sweeper. We agreed that only one of us should swim after him. Schilling and I suggested Hotten Sonntag, but he preferred to lie with Tulla Pokriefke behind the sun screen of the family beach and sprinkle sand on frogs' legs. Schilling claimed to have eaten too much breakfast: 'Eggs and all. My grandma from Krampitz has chickens and some Sundays she brings in two or three dozen eggs.'

I could think of no excuse. I rarely observed the rule about fasting before Communion and I had eaten breakfast very early. Besides, it was neither Schilling nor Hotten Sonntag who had said 'The Great Mahlke', but I. So I swam after him, in no particular hurry.

Tulla Pokriefke wanted to swim along with me, and we almost came to blows on the pier between the ladies' beach and the family beach. All arms and legs, she was sitting on the railing. Summer after summer she had been wearing that same mouse-grey, grossly darned child's bathing suit; what little bosom she had was crushed, elastic cut into her thighs, and between her legs the threadbare wool moulded itself in an intimate dimple. Curling her nose and spreading her toes, she screamed at me. When in return for some present or other – Hotten Sonntag was whispering in her ear – she agreed to withdraw, three or four little Third Formers, good swimmers, whom I had often seen on the barge, came climbing over the railing; they must have caught some of our conversation, for they wanted to swim to the barge though they didn't admit it. 'Oh no,' they protested, 'we're going somewhere else. Out to the breakwater. Or just to take a look.' Hotten Sonntag attended to them: 'Anybody that swims after him gets his balls polished.'

After a shallow dive from the pier I started off, changing my stroke frequently and taking my time. As I swam and as I write, I tried and I try to think of Tulla Pokriefke, for I didn't and still don't want to think of Mahlke. That's why I swam breaststroke, and that's why I write that I swam breaststroke. That was the only way I could see Tulla Pokriefke sitting on the railing, a bag of bones in – mouse-grey wool: and as I thought of her, she became smaller, crazier, more painful; for Tulla was a thorn in our flesh – but when I had the second sandbank

76

behind me, she was gone, thorn and dimple had passed the vanishing point, I was no longer swimming away from Tulla, but swimming toward Mahlke, and it is toward you that I write: I swam breaststroke and I didn't hurry.

I may as well tell you between two strokes – the water will hold me up – that this was the last Sunday before the summer holidays. What was going on at the time? They had occupied the Crimea, and Rommel was advancing again in North Africa. Since Easter we had been in the Upper Second. Esch and Hotten Sonntag had volunteered, both for the Air Force, but later on, just like me who kept hesitating whether to go into the Navy or not, they were sent to the Panzer Grenadiers, a kind of high-class infantry. Mahlke didn't volunteer, as usual he was the exception. 'You must be nuts,' he said. However, he was a year older, and there was every likelihood that he would be taken before we were; but a writer mustn't get ahead of himself.

I swam the last couple of hundred yards all in breast-stroke, but still more slowly in order to save my breath. The Great Mahlke was sitting as usual in the shadow of the pilot house. Only his knees were getting some sun. He must have been under once. The gargling remnants of an overture wavered in the fitful breeze and came out to meet me with the ripples. That was his way: dived down into his den, cranked up the gramophone, put on a record, came up with dripping watershed, sat down in the shade, and listened to his music while above him the screams of the gulls substantiated the doctrine of trans-migration.

No, not yet. Once again, before it is too late, let me turn over on my back and contemplate the great clouds shaped like potato sacks, which rose from Putziger Wiek and passed over our barge in endless procession, providing changes of light and cloud-long coolness. Never since – except at the exhibition of our local children's painting which Father Alban organized two years ago at our parish hall with my help, have I seen such beautiful, potato-sack-shaped clouds. And so once again, before the battered rust of the barge comes within reach, I ask: Why me? Why not Hotten Sonntag or Schilling? I might have sent the Third Formers, or Tulla with Hotten Sonntag. Or the whole lot of them including Tulla, for the Third Formers, especially one of them who seems to have been related to her, were always chasing after the little bag of bones. But no, bidding Schilling to make sure that no one followed me, I swam alone. And took my time.

I, Pilenz – what has my first name got to do with it? – formerly an altar boy dreaming of every imaginable future, now the parish hall secretary, just can't let magic alone; I read Bloy, the Gnostics, Böll, Friedrich Heer, and often with profound emotion the *Confessions* of good old St Augustine. Over tea brewed much too black, I spend whole nights discussing the blood of Christ, the Trinity, and divine penance with the Franciscan Father Alban, who is an open-minded man though more or less a believer. I tell him about Mahlke and Mahlke's Virgin, Mahlke's throat and Mahlke's aunt, Mahlke's sugar water, the parting in the middle of his hair, his gramophone, snowy owl, screwdriver, woollen pompoms, luminous buttons, about cat and mouse and *mea culpa*. I tell him how the Great Mahlke sat on the barge and I, taking my time, swam out to him alternating between breaststroke and backstroke; for I alone could be termed his friend, if it was possible to be friends with Mahlke. Anyway I made every effort. But why speak of effort? To me it was perfectly natural to trot along beside him and his changing attributes. If Mahlke had said: 'Do this and that,' I would have done this and that and much more. But Mahlke said nothing. I ran after him, I went

78

out of my way to pick him up on Osterzeile for the privilege of going to school by his side. And he merely put up with my presence without a word or a sign. When he introduced the pompom vogue, I was the first to take it up and wear pompoms on my neck. For a while, though only at home, I even wore a screwdriver on a shoelace. And if I continued to gratify Gusewski with my services as an altar boy, it was only in order to gaze at Mahlke's neck during holy communion. When in 1942, after Easter vacation – aircraft carriers were battling in the Coral Sea – the Great Mahlke shaved for the first time, I too began to scrape my chin, though no sign of a beard was discernible. And if after the submarine captain's speech Mahlke had said to me: 'Pilenz, go and swipe that thing on the ribbon,' I would have taken medal and ribbon off the hook and kept it for you.

But Mahlke attended to his own affairs. And now he was sitting in the shadow of the pilot house, listening to the tortured remains of his underwater music: *Cavalleria rusticana* – gulls overhead – the sea now smooth, now ruffled, now stirred by short-winded waves – two fat ships in the roadstead – scurrying cloud shadows – over toward Putzig a formation of speedboats: six bow waves, a few trawlers in between – I can already hear the gurgling of the barge, I swim slowly, breaststroke, look away, look beyond, in between the vestiges of the ventilators – I can't remember exactly how many – and before my hands grip the rust, I see you, as I've been seeing you for a good fifteen years: You! I swim, I grip the rust, I see You: the Great Mahlke sits impassive in the shadow, the gramophone record in the cellar catches, in love with a certain passage which it repeats till its breath fails; the gulls fly off; and there you are with the ribbon and *it* on your neck.

It was very funny looking, because he had nothing else on. He sat huddled, naked and bony in the shade with his eternal sunburn. Only the knees glared. His long, semi-relaxed cock and his testicles lay flat on the rust. His hands clutching his knees. His hair plastered in strands over his ears but still parted in the middle. And that face, that redeemer's countenance! And below it, motionless, his one and only article of clothing, the large, the enormous medal a hand's breadth below his collarbone.

For the first time the Adam's apple which, as I still believe – though he had auxiliary motors – was Mahlke's motor and brake, had found its exact counterweight. Quietly it slumbered beneath his skin. For a time it had no need to move, for the harmonious cross that soothed it had a long history; it had been designed in the year 1813, when iron was worth its weight in gold, by good old Schinkel who knew how to capture the eye with classical forms: slight changes in 1871, slight changes in 1914-18, and now again slight changes. But it bore no resemblance to the *Pour le Mérite*, a development of the Maltese Cross, although now for the first time, Schinkel's brainchild moved from chest to neck, proclaiming symmetry as a Credo.

'Hey, Pilenz! What do you think of my trinket? Not bad, eh?'

'Terrific! Let me touch it.'

'You'll admit I earned it.'

'I knew right away that you'd done the job.'

'Job nothing. It was conferred on me only yesterday for sinking five ships on the Murmansk run plus a cruiser of the *Southampton* class. . . .'

Both of us determined to make a show of lightheartedness, we grew very silly, bawled out every single verse of 'We're sailing against England,' made up new verses, in which neither tankers nor troop transports were torpedoed amidships, but certain girls and teachers from Gudrun School, forming megaphones of our hands, we blared out special communiqués, announcing our sinkings in terms both highflown and obscene, and drummed on the deck with our fists and heels. The barge groaned and rattled, dry gull droppings were shaken loose, gulls returned, speedboats passed in the distance, beautiful white clouds drifted over us, light as trails of smoke, comings and goings, happiness, shimmering light, not a fish leapt out of the water, friendly weather; the jumping jack started up again, but not because of any crisis in the throat, but because he was alive all over and for the first time a little giddy, gone the redeemer's countenance. Wild with glee, he removed the article from his neck and held the ends of the ribbon over his hip bones with a mincing little gesture. While with his legs, shoulders and twisted head he performed a fairly comical imitation of a girl, but no particular girl, the great iron biscuit dangled in front of his private parts, concealed no more than a third of his John Thomas.

In between – your circus number was beginning to get on my nerves – I asked him if he meant to keep the thing; it might be best, I suggested, to store it in his basement under the bridge, along with snowy owl, gramophone and Pilsudski.

The Great Mahlke had other plans and carried them out. For if Mahlke had stowed the object below decks; or better still, if I had never been friends with Mahlke; or still better, both at once: the object safe in the radio shack and I only vaguely interested in Mahlke, out of curiosity or because he was a classmate – then I should not have to write now and I should not have to say to Father Alban: 'Was it my fault if Mahlke later . . . ' As it is, I can't help writing, for you can't keep such things to yourself. Of course it is pleasant to pirouette on white paper – but what help are white clouds, soft breezes, speedboats coming in on schedule, and a flock of gulls doing the work of a Greek chorus; what good can any magical effects of syntax do me; even if I drop capitals and punctuation, I shall still have to say that Mahlke did not stow his bauble in the former radio shack of the former Polish mine sweeper *Rybitwa*, that he did not hang it between Marshal Pilsudski and the black Madonna, over the moribund gramophone and the decomposing snowy owl, that he went down under with his trinket on his neck, but stayed barely half an hour, while I counted sea-gulls, preening himself – I can swear to that – with his prize piece for the Virgin's benefit. I shall have to say that he brought it up again through the fo'c'sle hatch and was wearing it as he slipped on his trunks and swam back to the bathhouse with me at a good steady pace, that holding his treasure in his clenched fist, he smuggled it past Schilling, Hotten Sonntag, Tulla Pokriefke, and the Thirds, into his cabin in the gentlemen's section.

I was in no mood for talking and gave Tulla and her entourage only half an idea of what was up before vanishing into my cabin. I dressed quickly and caught Mahlke at the No. 9 tram stop. Throughout the ride I tried to persuade him, if it had to be, to return the medal personally to the lieutenant commander, whose address it would have been easy to find out.

I don't think he was listening. We stood on the rear platform, wedged in among the late Sunday morning crowd. From one stop to the next he opened his hand between his shirt and mine, and we both looked down at the severe dark metal with the rumpled, still wet ribbon. When we reached Saspe Manor, Mahlke held the medal over the knot of his tie, and tried to use the platform window as a mirror. As long as the tram stood motionless, waiting for the tram in the opposite direction to pass, I looked out over one of his ears, over the tumbledown Saspe cemetery, in the direction of the airfield. I was in luck: a large tri-motored Ju 52 was circling cautiously to a landing. That helped me.

Yet it was doubtful whether the Sunday crowd in the

car had eyes to spare for the Great Mahlke's exhibition. Amid benches and bundles of beach equipment, they were kept busy struggling with small children worn out from bathing. The whining and blubbering of children, rising, falling, rising, squelched, and ebbing off into sleep, echoed from the front to the rear platform and back – not to mention smells that would have turned the sweetest milk sour.

At the terminus in Brunshöferweg we got out and Mahlke said over his shoulder that he was planning to disturb the noonday repose of Dr Waldemar Klohse, our principal, that he was going in alone and there was no point in my waiting for him.

Klohse – as we all knew – lived in Baumbachallee. I accompanied the Great Mahlke through the tiled underpass, then I let him go his way; he did not hurry, I would even say that he zigzagged slightly. He held the ends of the ribbon between thumb and forefinger of his left hand; the medal twirled, serving as a propeller on his course to Baumbachallee.

An infernal idea! And why did he have to carry it out! If you had only thrown the damn thing up into the linden trees: in that residential quarter full of shade-dispensing foliage there were plenty of magpies that would have carried it off to their secret store, and tucked it away with the silver teaspoon, the ring and the brooch and the heap of gewgaws.

Mahlke was absent on Monday. The room was full of rumours. Dr Brunies conducted his German class, incorrigibly sucking the Cebion tablets he should have distributed to his pupils. Eichendorff lay open before him. Sweet and sticky his old man's mumble came to us from the desk: a few pages from the *Scamp*, then poems: *The Mill Wheel, The Little Ring, The Troubadour* – Two hearty journeymen went forth – If there's a fawn you love the

best – The song that slumbers in all things – Mild blows
the breeze and blue. Not a word about Mahlke.

It was not until Tuesday that Klohse came in with a
grey portfolio, and took his stance beside Dr Erdmann,
who rubbed his hands in embarrassment. Over our heads
resounded Klohse's cool breath: a disgraceful thing had
happened, and in these fateful times when we must all pull
together. The student in question – Klohse did not mention
the name – had already been removed from the establish-
ment. It had been decided, however, that other authorities,
the district bureau for example, would not be notified.
In the interests of the school the students were urged to
observe a manly silence, which alone could minimize the
effects of such scandalous behaviour. Such was the desire
of a distinguished alumnus, the lieutenant commander
and U-boat captain, bearer of the and so on. . . .

And so Mahlke was expelled, but – during the war
scarcely anyone was thrown out of secondary school for
good – transferred to the Horst-Wessel School, where his
story was kept very quiet.

Chapter Nine

The Horst-Wessel School, which before the war had been
called the Crown Prince Wilhelm School, was charac-
terized by the same dusty smell as our Conradinum. The
building, built in 1912, I think, seemed friendlier than our
brick edifice, but only on the outside. It was situated on
the southern edge of the suburb, at the foot of Jeschkental
Forest; consequently Mahlke's way to school and my way
to school did not intersect at any point when school
resumed in the autumn.

But there was no sign of him during the summer holidays either – a summer without Mahlke! – the story was

84

that he had signed up for a preliminary training camp offering courses in radio operation. His displayed his sunburn neither in Brösen nor at Glettkau Beach. Since there was no point in looking for him at St Mary's Chapel, Father Gusewski was deprived of one of his most reliable altar boys. Altar Boy Pilenz said to himself: No Mahlke, no Mass.

The rest of us lounged about the barge from time to time, but without enthusiasm. Hotten Sonntag tried in vain to find the way into the radio shack. Even the Third Formers had heard rumours of an amazing and amazingly furnished hideaway inside the bridge. A character with eyes very close together, whom the infants submissively addressed as Störtebeker, dived indefatigably. Tulla Pokriefke's cousin, a rather sickly little fellow, came out to the barge once or twice, but never dived. Either in my thoughts or in reality I try to strike up a conversation with him about Tulla; I was interested in her. But she had ensnared her cousin as she had me – what with, I wonder? With her threadbare wool, with her ineradicable smell of carpenter's glue? 'It's none of your bloody business!' That's what the cousin said to me – or might have.

Tulla didn't swim out to the barge; she stayed on the beach, but she had given up Hotten Sonntag. I took her to the movies twice, but even so I had no luck; she'd go to the movies with anybody. It was said that she had fallen for Störtebeker, but if so her love was unrequited, for Störtebeker had fallen for our barge and was looking for the entrance to Mahlke's hideout. As the vacation drew to an end there was a good deal of whispering to the effect that his diving had been successful. But there was never any proof: he produced neither a waterlogged gramophone record nor a decaying owl feather. Still, the rumours persisted; and when, two and a half years later, the so-called Dusters, a somewhat mysterious gang supposedly led by Störtebeker, were arrested, our barge and the hiding place under the bridge appear to have been mentioned. But by then I was in the Army; all I heard was a line or two in letters – for until the end, or rather as long as the mails were running, Father Gusewski wrote me letters ranging from pastoral to friendly. In one of the last, written in January '45 – as the Russian armies were approaching Elbing – there was something about a scandalous assault of the Dusters on the Church of the Sacred Heart, where Father Wiehnke officiated. In this letter Störtebeker was referred to by his real name; and it also seems to me that I read something about a three-year-old child whom the gang had cherished as a kind of mascot. I am pretty certain, though sometimes I have my doubts, that in his last or next to last letter – I lost the whole packet and my diary as well near Cottbus – there was some mention of the barge which had its big day before the onset of the summer vacation of '42, but whose glory paled in the course of the summer; for to this day that summer has a flat taste in my mouth – what was summer without Mahlke?

Not that we were really unhappy about his absence. I myself was glad to be rid of him, so I didn't have to chase after him the whole time; but why, I wonder, did I report to Father Gusewski as soon as school began again, offering my services at the altar? The reverend father's eyes crinkled with delight behind his rimless glasses and grew smooth and solemn behind the selfsame glasses only when – we were sitting in the sacristy and I was brushing his cassock – I asked, as though in passing, about Joachim Mahlke. Calmly, raising one hand to his glasses, he declared: 'Yes, yes, he is still one of the most faithful members of my congregation; never misses a Sunday Mass. You know, I presume, that he was away for four weeks, at a so-called pre-military training camp; but I shouldn't like to think that you're coming back to us only on Mahlke's account. Speak up, Pilenz!'

Exactly two weeks earlier, we had received news that my brother Klaus, a sergeant in the army, had fallen in the Kuban. I spoke of his death as my reason for wishing to resume my duties as an altar boy. Father Gusewski seemed to believe me; at any rate he tried to believe in me and my renewed piety.

I don't recollect the particulars of Winter's or Hotten Sonntag's face. But Father Gusewski had thick wavy hair, black with the barest sprinkling of grey, which could be counted on to sprinkle his cassock with dandruff. Meticulously tonsured, the crown of his head had a bluish glint. He gave off an aroma compounded of hair tonic and Palmolive soap. Sometimes he smoked Turkish cigarettes in an ornately carved amber holder. He enjoyed a reputation for progressiveness and played pingpong in the sacristy with the altar boys and those preparing for their first communion. He liked the ecclesiastical linen, the humeral and the alb, to be immoderately starched, a chore attended to by a certain Mrs Tolkmit or, when the old lady was ailing, by a handy altar boy, often myself. He himself appended sachets of lavender to every maniple, every stole, to all the Mass vestments, whether they lay in chests or hung in closets. Once when I was about thirteen, he ran his small, hairless hand down my back under my shirt from my neck to the waist of my gym shorts, but stopped there because my shorts had no elastic band and I tied them in front with tapes. I didn't give the incident much thought, for Father Gusewski had won my sympathy with his friendly, often boyish ways. I can still remember his ironic benevolence; so not another word about the occasional wanderings of his hand; all perfectly harmless, it was really my Catholic soul he was looking for. All in all, he was a priest like hundreds of others; he maintained a well-selected library for a working-class congregation that read little; his zeal was not excessive, his belief had its limits – in regard to the Assumption, for instance – and he always spoke, whether over the corporal about the blood of Christ or in the sacristy about ping-pong, in the same tone of unctuous serenity. It did strike me as silly when early in 1940 he put in a petition to have his name changed – less than a year later he called himself, and had others call him, Father Gusewing. But the fashion for Germanizing Polish sounding names ending in *ki* or *ke* or *a* – like Formella – was taken up by lots of people in those days: Lewandowski became Lengnisch; Mr Olczewski, our butcher, had himself metamorphosed into a Mr Ohlwein; Jürgen Kupka's parents wanted to take the East Prussian name of Kupkat, but their petition, heaven knows why, was rejected. Perhaps in emulation of one Saul who became Paul, a certain Gusewski wished to become Gusewing – but in these papers Father Gusewski will continue to be Gusewski; for you, Joachim Mahlke, did not change your name.

When for the first time after summer vacation I served early Mass at the altar, I saw him again and anew. Immediately after the prayers at the foot of the altar – Father Gusewski stood on the Epistle side and was busy with the introitus – I sighted him in the second pew, before the altar of Our Lady. But it was only between the reading of the Epistle and the gradual, and more freely during the Gospel reading, that I found time to examine his appearance. His hair was still parted in the middle and still held in place with the usual sugar water; but he wore it a good inch longer. Stiff and candied, it fell over his two ears like the two sides of a steep pointed roof: he would have made a satisfactory Jesus the way he held up his joined hands on a level with his forehead without propping his elbows; beneath them I perceived a bare, unguarded neck that concealed none of its secrets; for he was wearing his shirt collar open and folded on his jacket collar in the manner hallowed by Schiller: no tie, no pompoms, no pendants, no screwdriver nor any other item from his copious arsenal. The only heraldic beast in an otherwise vacant field was the restless mouse which he harboured under his skin in place of a larynx, which had once attracted a cat and had tempted me to put the cat on his neck. The area between Adam's apple and chin was still marked with a few crusty razor cuts. At the *Sanctus* I almost came in too late with the bell.

At the communion rail Mahlke's attitude was less affected. His joined hands dropped down below his collarbone and his mouth smelled as though a pot of cabbage were simmering on a small flame within him. Once he had his wafer, another daring innovation captured my attention: in former days Mahlke, like every other communicant, had returned directly from the communion rail to his place in the second row of pews; now he prolonged and interrupted this silent itinerary, first striding slowly and stiffly to the middle of the altar of Our Lady, then falling on both knees, not on the linoleum floor but on a shaggy carpet which began shortly before the altar steps. Then he raised his joined hands until they were level with his eyes, with the parting in his hair, and higher still he held them out in supplication and yearning to the over-life-size plaster figure which stood childless, a virgin among virgins, on a silver-plated crescent moon, draped from shoulders to ankles in a Prussian-blue starry mantle, her long-fingered hands folded over her flat bosom, gazing with slightly protuberant glass eyes at the ceiling of the former gymnasium. When Mahlke arose knee after knee and reassembled his hands in front of his Schiller collar, the carpet had imprinted a coarse, bright-red pattern on his kneecaps.

Father Gusewski had also observed certain aspects of Mahlke's new style. Not that I asked questions. Quite of his own accord, as though wishing to throw off or to share a burden, he began immediately after Mass to speak of

89

Mahlke's excessive zeal, of his dangerous attachment to outward forms. Yes, Father Gusewski was worried; it had seemed to him for some time that regardless of what inner affliction brought Mahlke to the altar, his cult of the Virgin bordered on pagan idolatry.

He was waiting for me at the door of the sacristy. I was so frightened I almost ran back in again, but at once he took my arm, laughed in a free and easy way that was completely new, and talked and talked. He who had formerly been so monosyllabic spoke about the weather – Indian summer, threads of gold in the air. And then abruptly, but in the same conversational tone and without even lowering his voice: 'I've volunteered. I can't understand it. You know how I feel about all that stuff: militarism, playing soldier, the current overemphasis on martial virtues. Guess what branch of service. Don't make me laugh. The Air Force is all washed up. Paratroopers? Wrong again! Why wouldn't you think of the submarines? Well, at last! That's the only branch that still has a chance. Though of course I'll feel like an ass in one of those things and I'd rather do something useful or funny. You remember I wanted to be a clown. Lord, what ideas a kid can get!

'I still think it's a pretty good idea. Otherwise things aren't so bad. Dammit all, school is school. What mad ideas I used to have. Do you remember? Just couldn't get used to this bump. I thought it was some kind of disease. But it's perfectly normal. I've known people, or at least I've seen some, with still bigger ones; they don't get upset. The whole thing started that day with the cat. You remember. We were lying in Heinrich-Ehlers Field. A Schlagball tournament was going on. I was sleeping or daydreaming, and that grey beast, or was it black? saw my neck and jumped, or one of you, Schilling I think, it's the kind of thing he would do, took the cat. . . . Well, that's ancient history. No, I haven't been back to the barge. Störtebeker?

Never heard of him. Let him, let him. I don't own the barge, do I? Come and see us soon.'

It was not until the third Sunday of Advent – all that autumn Mahlke had made me a model altar boy – that I accepted his invitation. Until Advent I had been obliged to serve all by myself. Father Gusewski had been unable to find a second altar boy. Actually I had wanted to visit Mahlke on the first Sunday of Advent and bring him a candle, but the shipment came too late and it was not until the second Sunday that Mahlke was able to place the consecrated candle on the altar of the Virgin. 'Can you rustle up some?' he had asked me. 'Gusewski won't give me any.' I said that I'd do what I could, and actually succeeded in procuring one of those long candles, pale as potato shoots, that are so rare in wartime; for my brother's death entitled my family to a candle. I went on foot to the rationing office and they gave me a coupon after I had submitted the death certificate. Then I took the streetcar to the religious articles shop in Oliva, but they were out of candles. I had to go back again and then a sceond time, and so it was only on the second Sunday of Advent that I was able to give you your candle and see you kneel with it at the altar of Our Lady, as I had long dreamed of seeing you. Gusewski and I wore violet for Advent. But your neck sprouted from a white Schiller collar which was not obscured by the reversed and remodelled overcoat you had inherited from an engine driver killed in an accident, for you no longer – another innovation! – wore a muffler fastened with a large safety pin.

And Mahlke knelt stiffly and at length on the coarse carpet on the second Sunday of Advent and again on the third, the day I decided to take him at his word and drop in on him in the afternoon. His glassy unquivering gaze – or if it quivered, it was when I was busy at the altar – was aimed over the candle at the belly of the Mother of God.

His hands formed a steep roof over his forehead and its thoughts, but he did not touch his forehead with his crossed thumbs.

And I thought: today I'll go. I'll go and take a look at him. I'll study him. Yes, so I will. There must be something behind all that – Besides, he had invited me.

Osterzeile was a short street: and yet the one-family houses with their empty trellises against house fronts scrubbed till they were sore, the uniform trees along the sidewalks – the lindens had lost their poles within the last year but still required props – discouraged and wearied me, although our Westerzeile was identical, or perhaps it was because our Westerzeile had the same smell and celebrated the seasons with the same lilliputian garden plots. Even today when, as rarely happens, I leave the settlement house to visit friends or acquaintances in Stockum or Lohhausen, between the airfield and the North Cemetery, and have to pass through streets of housing development which repeat themselves just as wearisomely and dishearteningly from house number to house number, from linden to linden, I am still on the way to visit Mahlke's mother and Mahlke's aunt and you, the Great Mahlke; the bell is fastened to a garden gate that I might have stepped over without effort, just by stretching my legs a little. Steps through the wintry but snowless front garden with its top-heavy rosebushes wrapped for the winter. The flowerless flowerbeds are decorated with Baltic sea-shells broken and intact. The ceramic tree frog the size of a rabbit is seated on a slag of rough marble embedded in crusty garden soil that has crumbled over it in places. And in the flowerbed on the other side of the narrow path which, while I think of it, guides me from the garden gate to the three brick steps before the ochre-stained, round-arched door, stands, just across from the tree frog, an almost vertical pole some five feet high,

92

topped with a bird house in the Alpine manner. The sparrows go on eating as I negotiate the seven or eight paces between flowerbed and flowerbed. It might be supposed that the development smells fresh, clean sandy and seasonal – but Osterzeile, Westerzeile, Bärenweg, no the whole of Langfuhr, West Prussia, or Germany for that matter, smelled in those war years of onions, onions stewing in margarine; I won't try to determine what else was stewing, but one thing that could always be identified was freshly chopped onions, although onions were scarce and hard to come by, although jokes about the onion shortage, in connexion with Field Marshal Goering, who had said something or other about short onions on the radio, were going the rounds in Langfuhr, in West Prussia, and all over Germany. Perhaps if I rubbed my typewriter superficially with onion juice, it might communicate an intimation of the onion smell which in those years contaminated all Germany, West Prussia and Langfuhr, Osterzeile as well as Westerzeile, preventing the smell of corpses from taking over completely.

I took the three brick steps at one stride, and my curved hand was preparing to grasp the door handle when the door was opened from within – by Mahlke in Schiller collar and felt slippers. He must have refurbished the parting in his hair a short while before. Neither light nor dark, in rigid, freshly combed strands, it slanted backwards in both directions from the parting. Still impeccably neat; but when I left an hour later, it had begun to quiver as he spoke and droop over his large flamboyant ears.

We sat in the rear of the house, in the living room which received its light from the jutting glass veranda. There was cake made from some war recipe, potato cake, the predominant taste was rose water, which was supposed to awaken memories of marzipan. Afterwards preserved plums which had a normal taste and had ripened during

93

the fall in Mahlke's garden – the tree, leafless and with whitewashed trunk, could be seen in the left-hand pane of the veranda. My chair was assigned to me: I was at the narrow end of the table, looking out, while Mahlke, opposite me at the other end, had the veranda behind him. To the left of me, illumined from the side so that grey hair curled silvery, Mahlke's aunt; to the right, her right side illumined, but less glittering because combed more tightly, Mahlke's mother. Although the room was over-heated, it was a cold wintry light that outlined the fuzzy edges of her ears and a few trembling wisps of loose hair. The wide Schiller collar gleamed whiter than white at the top, blending into grey lower down: Mahlke's neck lay flat in the shadow.

The two women were rawboned, born and raised in the country. They were at a loss what to do with their hands and spoke profusely, never at the same time, but always in the direction of Joachim Mahlke even when they were addressing me and asking about my mother's health. They both spoke to me through him, who acted as our interpreter: 'So now your brother Klaus is dead. I knew him only by sight, but what a handsome boy!'

Mahlke was a mild but firm chairman. When the questions became too personal – while my father was sending APO letters from Greece, my mother was indulging in intimate relations, mostly with non-coms – well, Mahlke warded off questions in that direction: 'Never mind about that, Auntie. Who can afford to judge in times like this when everything is topsy-turvy. Besides, it is really no business of yours, Mama. If Papa were still alive, he wouldn't like it, he wouldn't let you speak like that.'

Both women obeyed him or else they obeyed the departed engine driver whom he quietly conjured up whenever his aunt or mother began to gossip. When they spoke of the situation at the front – confusing the battle-fields of Russia with those of North Africa, saying El

Alamein when they meant the Sea of Azov – Mahlke managed quietly, without irritation, to guide the conversation into the right geographical channels: 'No, Auntie, that naval battle was at Guadalcanal, not in Karelia.'

Nevertheless, his aunt had given the cue and we lost ourselves in conjectures about the Japanese and American aircraft carriers that may have been sunk off Guadalcanal. Mahlke believed that the carriers *Hornet* and *Wasp*, the keels of which had been laid only in 1939, as well as the *Ranger*, had been completed in time to take part in the battle, for either the *Saratoga* or the *Lexington*, perhaps both, had meanwhile been sunk. We were still more in the dark about the two big Japanese carriers, the *Akagi* and the *Kaga*, which was decidedly too slow to be effective. Mahlke expressed daring opinions; only aircraft carriers, he said, would figure in the naval battles of the future, there was no longer any point in building battleships, it was the small, fast craft and the carriers that counted. He went into details. When he rattled off the names of the Italian *esploratori*, both women gaped in amazement and Mahlke's aunt clapped her bony hands resoundingly; there was something girlish about her enthusiasm, and in the silence that followed her clapping, she fiddled with her hair in embarrassment.

Not a word fell about the Horst-Wessel School. I almost seem to remember that as I was getting up to go, Mahlke laughingly mentioned his old nonsense about his neck, as he put it, and even went so far – his mother and aunt joined in the laughter – as to tell the story about the cat: this time it was Jürgen Kupka who put the cat on his throat; if only I knew who made up the story, he or I, or who is writing this in the first place!

In any case – this much is certain – his mother found some wrapping paper and packed up two little pieces of potato cake for me as I was taking my leave. In the hall, beside the staircase leading to the upper storey and his attic, Mahlke pointed out a photograph hanging beside the brush bag. The whole landscape width was taken up with a rather modern looking locomotive with tender, belonging to the Polish railways – the letters PKP could be clearly distinguished in two places. In front of the engine stood two men, tiny but imposing, with folded arms. The Great Mahlke said: 'My father and Lubada the fireman, shortly before they were killed in an accident near Dirschau in '34. But my father managed to prevent the whole train from being wrecked; they awarded him a medal posthumously.'

Chapter Ten

Early in the New Year I thought I would take violin lessons – my brother had left a violin – but we were enrolled as Air Force auxiliaries and today it is probably too late although Father Alban keeps telling me that I ought to. And it was he who encouraged me to write about Cat and Mouse: 'Just sit yourself down, my dear Pilenz, and start writing. Yes, yes, there was too much Kafka in your first poetic efforts and short stories, but even so, you've got a style of your own: if you won't take up the fiddle, you can get it off your chest by writing – the good Lord knew what he was doing when he gave you talent.'

So we were enrolled in the Brösen-Glettkau shore battery, or training battery if you will, behind the gravel-strewn beach promenade, amid dunes and blowing beach grass, in buildings that smelled of tar, socks and the beach grass used to stuff our mattresses. There might be lots of things to say about the daily life of an Air Force auxiliary, a schoolboy in uniform, subjected in the morning to grey-haired teachers and the traditional methods of

96

education and in the afternoon obliged to memorize gunnery instructions and the secrets of ballistics; but this is not the place to tell my story, or the story of Hotten Sonntag's simple-minded vigour, or to recount the utterly commonplace adventures of Schilling – here I am speaking only of you; and Joachim Mahlke never became an Air Force auxiliary.

Just in passing and without trying to tell a coherent story beginning with cat and mouse, some students from the Horst-Wessel School, who were also being trained in the Brösen-Glettkau shore battery, contributed a certain amount of new material: 'Just after Christmas they drafted him into the Reich Labour Service. Oh yes, he graduated, they gave him the special wartime diploma. Hell, examinations were never any problem for him, he was quite a bit older than the rest of us. They say his battalion is out on Tuchler Heath. Cutting peat maybe. They say things are happening up there. Partisans and so on.'

In February I went to see Esch at the Air Force hospital in Oliva. He was lying there with a fractured collarbone and wanted cigarettes. I gave him some and he treated me to some sticky liqueur. I didn't stay long. On the way to the streetcar bound for Glettkau I made a detour through the Castle Park. I wanted to see whether the good old whispering grotto was still there. It was: some convalescent Alpine troops were trying it out with the nurses, whispering at the porous stone from both sides, tittering, whispering, tittering. I had no one to whisper with and went off, with some plan or other in mind, down a birdless, perhaps brambly path which led straight from the castle pond and whispering grotto to the Zoppot highway. It was rather like a tunnel because of the bare branches that joined overhead and it kept growing frighteningly narrower. I passed two nurses leading a hobbling, laughing, hobbling lieutenant, then two grandmothers and a little boy who might have been three years old, didn't want to be connected with the grandmothers and was carrying but not beating a child's drum. Then out of the February-grey tunnel of brambles, something else approached and grew larger: Mahlke.

We were both ill at ease. There was something eerie, almost awesome about a meeting on such a path without forks or byways, cut off even from the sky: it was fate or the Rococo fantasy of a French landscape architect that had brought us together – and to this day I avoid inextricable castle parks designed in the manner of good old Le Nôtre.

Of course a conversation started up, but I couldn't help staring transfixed at his head covering; for the Labour Service cap, even when worn by others than Mahlke, was unequalled for ugliness: a crown of disproportionate height sagged forward over the peak; the whole was saturated with the colour of dried excrement; the crown was creased in the middle in the manner of a civilian hat, but the bulges were closer together, so close as to produce the plastic furrow which explains why the Labour Service head covering was commonly referred to as 'an arse with a handle'. On Mahlke's head this hat made a particularly painful impression, for it seemed to accentuate the very same parting in the middle which the Labour Service had forced him to give up. We were both of us on edge as we stood facing one another between and beneath the brambles. And then the little boy came back without the grandmothers, pounding his tin drum, circumnavigated us in a semicircle with magical overtones, and at last vanished down the tapering path with his noise.

We exchanged a hasty goodbye after Mahlke had tersely and morosely answered my questions about fighting with partisans on Tuchler Heath, about the food in the Labour Service, and as to whether any Labour Service Maidens were stationed near them. I also wanted to know

98

what he was doing in Oliva and whether he had been to see Father Gusewski. I learned that the food was tolerable, but that he had seen no sign of any Labour Service Maidens. He thought the rumours about fighting with partisans to be exaggerated but not entirely unfounded. His commander had sent him to Oliva for some spare parts: official business, justifying a two days' absence. 'I spoke to Gusewski this morning, right after early Mass.' Then a disparaging wave of the hand: 'Hell can freeze over, he'll always be the same!' and the distance between us increased, because we were taking steps.

No, I didn't look after him. Unbelievable, you think? But if I say 'Mahlke didn't turn around in my direction,' you won't doubt me. Several times I had to look behind me because there was no one, not even the little boy with his noise box, coming towards me to help.

Then as I figure it, I didn't see you for a whole year; but not to see you was not, and still is not, to forget you and your fearful symmetry. Besides there were reminders: If I saw a cat, whether grey or black or pepper-and-salt, the mouse ran into my field of vision forthwith; but still I hesitated, undecided whether the mouse should be protected or the cat goaded into catching it.

Until summer we lived at the shore battery, played endless games of handball, and on visiting Sundays rollicked to the best of our ability in the beach thistles, always with the same girls or their sisters; I alone accomplished nothing at all. Hesitation was my trouble; I haven't got over it yet, and this weakness of mine still inspires me with the same ironical reflections. What else occupied our days? Distributions of peppermint drops, lectures about venereal diseases; in the morning *Hermann and Dorothea*, in the afternoon the 98-K rifle, mail, four-fruit jam, singing contests. In our hours off duty we sometimes swam out to our barge, where we regularly found swarms of the little Third Formers who were coming up after us and who irritated us no end, and as we swam back we couldn't for the life of us understand what for three summers had so attached us to that mass of rust encrusted with gull droppings. Later we were transferred to the 88-millimetre battery in Pelonken and then to the Zigankenberg battery. There were three or four alerts and our battery helped to shoot down a four-motor bomber. For weeks several orderly rooms submitted rival claims to the accidental hit – and through it all, peppermint drops, *Hermann and Dorothea*, and lots of saluting.

Because they had volunteered for the army, Hotten Sonntag and Esch were sent to the Labour Service even sooner than I. Hesitating as usual, unable to make up my mind which branch of service I favoured, I had missed the deadline for volunteering. In February 1944, with a good half of our class, I took and passed the final examinations – which differed little from the usual peacetime variety – and promptly received notice to report for Labour Service. Discharged from the Air Force Auxiliaries, I had a good two weeks ahead of me and was determined to do something conclusive in addition to winning my diploma. Whom did I light on but Tulla Pokriefke, who was sixteen or over and very accessible, but I had no luck and didn't get anywhere with Hotten Sonntag's sister either. In this situation and state of mind – I was comforted to some extent by letters from one of my cousins; the whole family had been evacuated to Silesia after an air raid had left their house a total loss – I made a farewell visit to Father Gusewski, promised to help at the altar during the leaves I hoped I would get, and was given a new Missal and a handy metal crucifix, specially manufactured for Catholic recruits. Then at the corner of Bärenweg and Osterzeile on my way home, I ran into Mahlke's aunt, who wore thick glasses when she went out and was not to be avoided.

Before we had even exchanged greetings, she began to

100

talk, at a good clip in spite of her rural drawl. When people came by, she gripped my shoulder and pulled until one of my ears approached her mouth. Hot, moist sentences. She began with irrelevant chit-chat. The shopping situation: 'You can't even get what you've got coupons for.' I learned that onions were not to be found, but that brown sugar and barley grits were obtainable at Matzerath's and that Ohlwein, the butcher, was expecting some canned pork. Finally, with no cue from me, she came to the point: 'The boy is better now, though he don't exactly say so in his letters. But he's never been one to complain, he's just like his father who was my brother-in-law. And now they've put him in the tanks. He'll be safer than in the infantry and dry when it rains.'

Then whispers crept into my ear and I learned of Mahlke's new eccentricities, of the infantile pictures he drew under the signature of his letters.

'The funny part of it is that he never drew when he was little, except for the water colours he had to make in school. But here's his last letter in my pocketbook. Dear, how rumpled it is! Oh, Mr Pilenz, there's so many people want to see how the boy is doing.'

And Mahlke's aunt showed me Mahlke's letter. 'Go ahead and read it.' But I didn't read. Paper between gloveless fingers. A dry, sharp wind came circling down from Max-Halbe-Platz and nothing could stop it. Battered my heart with the heel of its boot and tried to kick the door in. Seven brothers spoke within me, but none of them followed the writing. There was snow in the wind but I could still see the letter paper distinctly, though it was greyish-brown, poor quality. Today I may say that I understood immediately, but I just stared, wishing neither to look nor to understand; for even before the paper crackled close to my eyes, I had realized that Mahlke was starting up again: squiggly line drawings under neat Sütterlin script. In a row which he had taken

101

great pains to make straight, but which was nevertheless crooked because the paper was unlined, eight, twelve, thirteen, fourteen unequally flattened circles and on every kidney a wartlike knob, and from each wart a bar the length of a thumbnail, projecting beyond the lopsided boiler toward the left edge of the paper. And on each of these tanks – for clumsy as the drawings were, I recognized the Russian T-34 – there was a mark, mostly between turret and boiler, a cross indicating a hit. And in addition – evidently the artist didn't expect the viewers of his work to be very bright – all fourteen of the T-34s – yes, I'm pretty sure there were fourteen of them – were cancelled very emphatically with large crosses in blue pencil.

Quite pleased with myself, I explained to Mahlke's aunt that the drawings obviously represented tanks that Joachim had knocked out. But Mahlke's aunt didn't show the least surprise, plenty of people had already told her that, but what she couldn't understand was why there were sometimes more, sometimes less of them, once only eight and, in the letter before last, twenty-seven.

'Maybe it's because the mails are so irregular – But now, Mr Pilenz, you must read what our Joachim writes. He mentions you too, in connexion with candles, but we've already got some.' I barely skimmed through the letter: Mahlke was thoughtful, inquiring about all his aunt's and mother's major and minor ailments – the letter was addressed to both of them – varicose veins, pains in the back, and so on. He asked for news of the garden: 'Did the plum tree bear well this year? How are my cactuses doing?' Only a few words about his duties, which he called fatiguing and responsible: 'Of course we have our losses. But the Blessed Virgin will protect me as in the past.' Would his mother and aunt kindly give Father Gusewski one or if possible two candles for the altar of Our Lady? And then: 'Maybe Pilenz can get you some; they have coupons.' He furthermore asked them to offer prayers to

102

St Judas Thaddaeus – a nephew twice-removed of the Virgin Mary, Mahlke knew his Holy Family – and also have a Mass said for his late-lamented Father who 'left us without receiving the sacraments'. At the end of the letter, more trifles and some pale landscape painting: 'You can't imagine how run down everything is here, how wretched the people are and all the many children. No electricity or running water. Sometimes I begin to wonder what it's all for, but I suppose it has to be. And some day if you feel like it and the weather is good, take the tram out to Brösen – but dress warmly – and look out to the left of the harbour mouth, but not so far out, to see whether the superstructure of a sunken ship is still there. There used to be an old wreck there. You can see it with the naked eye and Auntie has her glasses – it would interest me to know if it's still . . . '

I said to Mahlke's aunt: 'You can spare yourself the ride. The barge is still in the same place. And give Joachim my best when you write. He can set his mind at rest, nothing changes around here, and nobody's likely to walk off with the barge.'

And even if the Schichau Shipyards had walked off with it, that is, raised it, scrapped or refitted it, would it have done you any good? Would you have stopped scribbling Russian tanks with childish precision on your letters and crossing them off in blue pencil? And who could have scrapped the Virgin? And who could have bewitched our good old School and turned it into bird seed? And the cat and the mouse? Are there stories that can cease to be?

Chapter Eleven

With Mahlke's scribbled testimonials before my eyes, I had to live through three more days at home. My mother was devoting her attentions to a construction foreman from the Todt Organization – or maybe she was still cooking the saltless diet dishes that found the way to Lieutenant Stiewe's heart – one of these gentlemen at any rate had made himself at home in our apartment and, apparently unaware of the symbolism of the thing, was wearing the slippers my father had broken in. In an atmosphere of cosy comfort that might have been cut out of a woman's magazine, my mother bustled from one room to the next in mourning; black was becoming to her, she wore it to go out and she wore it to stay in. On the sideboard she had erected a kind of altar for my fallen brother: first in a black frame and under glass a passport photo enlarged past recognition, showing him as a sergeant but without the peaked cap; second, similarly framed and covered with glass, the death notices from the *Vorposten* and the *Neueste Nachrichten*; third, she had tied up a packet of his letters in a black silk ribbon; to which, fourth, she had appended the Iron Crosses, first and second class, and the Crimean Medal, and placed the bundle to the left of the photographs; while fifth and on the right, my brother's violin and bow, resting on some music paper with notes on it – my brother had tried his hand at composing violin sonatas – formed a counter-weight to the letters.

If today I occasionally miss my elder brother Klaus, whom I scarcely knew, what I felt at the time was mostly jealousy on account of that altar; I visualized my own enlarged photo thus framed in black, felt slighted, and often chewed my fingernails when I was alone in our living room with my brother's altar, which refused to be ignored.

One fine morning as the lieutenant lay on the couch preoccupied with his stomach and my mother in the kitchen cooked saltless gruel, I would certainly have smashed that altar – photo, death notices, and perhaps the fiddle as well; my fist would have lost its temper without consulting me. But before that could happen, my departure date came, depriving me of a scene which would still be stageworthy: so well had death in the Kuban, my mother by the sideboard, and I, the great procrastinator, prepared the script. Instead, I marched off with my imitation leather suitcase, and took the train to Konitz via Berent. For three months between Osche and Reetz, I had occasion to familiarize myself with Tuchler Heath. Everywhere wind and sand. Spring days to gladden the hearts of insect lovers. Rolling, round juniper berries. Wherever you turned, bushes and things to take aim at: the idea was to hit the two cardboard soldiers behind the fourth bush on the left. Over the birches and butterflies beautiful clouds with no place to go. In the bogs, circular, shiny-dark ponds where you could fish with hand grenades for perch and moss-covered carp. Nature wherever you looked. And movies in Tuchel.

Nevertheless and in spite of birches, clouds and perch, I can give only a rough sketch, as in a sand tray, of this Labour Service battalion with its compound of shacks nestling in a copse, its flagpole, garbage pits, and off to one side of the school shack, its latrine. My only justification for telling you even this much is that a year before me, before Winter, Jürgen Kupka and Bansemer, the Great Mahlke had worn denims and clodhoppers in the same compound, and literally left his name behind him: in the latrine, a roofless wooden box plunked down amid the broom and the overhead murmuring of the scrub pines. Here the two syllables – no first name – were carved or rather chipped, into pine board across from the throne and below the name, in flawless Latin, but in an unrounded runic sort of script, the beginning of his favourite sequence: *Stabat mater dolorosa*. . . . The Franciscan monk Jacopone da Todi would have been so pleased, but all it meant to me was that even in the Labour Service I couldn't get rid of Mahlke. For while I relieved myself, while the maggot-ridden dross of my age group accumulated behind me and under me, you gave me and my eyes no peace: loudly and in breathless repetition, a painstakingly incised text called attention to Mahlke, whatever I might decide to whistle in opposition.

· And yet I am sure that Mahlke had had no intention of joking. Mahlke couldn't joke. He sometimes tried. But everything he did, touched or said, became solemn, significant, monumental; so also his runic inscription in the pine wood of a Reich Labour Service latrine named Tuchel-North, between Osche and Reetz. Digestive aphorisms, lines from lewd songs, crude or stylized anatomy – nothing helped. Mahlke's text drowned out all the more or less wittily formulated obscenities which, carved or scribbled from top to bottom of the latrine wall, gave tongues to wooden boards.

What with the accuracy of the quotation and the awesome secrecy of the place, I might almost have got religion in the course of time. And then this gloomy conscience of mine wouldn't be driving me to do underpaid social work in a settlement house, I wouldn't spend my time trying to discover early Communism in Nazareth or late Christianity in Ukrainian kolkhozes. I should at least be delivered from these all-night discussions with Father Alban, from trying to determine, in the course of endless investigations, to what extent blasphemy can take the place of prayer. I should be able to believe, to believe something, no matter what, perhaps even to believe in the resurrection of the flesh. But one day after I had been chopping kindling in

106

the battalion kitchen, I took the axe and hacked Mahlke's favourite sequence out of the board and eradicated your name.

It was the old story of the spot that found no takers, kind of grisly-moral and transcendent; for the empty patch of wood with its fresh fibres spoke more eloquently than the chipped inscription. Besides, your message must have spread with the shavings, for in the barracks, between kitchen, guardroom and dressing room, stories as tall as a house began to go round, especially on Sundays when boredom took to counting flies. The stories were always the same, varying only in minor detail. About a Labour Service Man named Mahlke, who had served a good year before in Tuchel-North battalion and must have done some mighty sensational things. Two truck drivers, the cook, and the room orderly had been there the whole time, every shipment had passed them by. Without significantly contradicting one another they spoke roughly as follows: 'This is how he looked the first day. Hair down to here. Well, they sent him to the barber. Don't make me laugh. He needed more than a barber: ears like an egg beater and a neck, a neck I tell you! He also had – and once when – for instance when he – but the most amazing thing about him was when I sent the whole pack of new recruits to Tuchel to be deloused because as room orderly I. . . . When they were all under the shower, I says to myself, my eyes are playing tricks on me, so I look again, and I says to myself, mustn't get envious now, but that cock of his, take it from me, a monster, when he got excited it would stand up to or maybe more, anyway he made good use of it with the commander's wife, a strapping piece in her forties, because the damn-fool commander – he's been transferred to France, a nut – sent him over to his house, the second from the left in Officers' Row, to build a rabbit hutch. At first Mahlke, that was his name, refused,

107

no he didn't fly off the handle, he just quietly quoted chapter and verse from the Service regulations. That didn't do him a bit of good. The chief personally chewed his bollocks till he could hardly – and for the next two days he was shovelling shit in the latrine. I hosed him off from a respectful distance, because the boys wouldn't let him into the washroom. Finally he gave in and went toddling over with tools and boards. All that fuss over rabbits! He must really have screwed that old lady! Every day for more than a week she sent for him to work in the garden; every morning Mahlke toddled off and was back again for roll call. But that rabbit hutch wasn't making any headway at all, so finally it dawned on the chief. I don't know if he caught them bare arsed, maybe on the kitchen table or maybe between the sheets like mama and papa, anyway, he must have been struck speechless when he saw Mahlke's, anyway he never said one word about it here in the barracks: it's not hard to see why. And he sent Mahlke off on official trips whenever he could to Oliva and Oxhöft for spare parts, just to get that stud and his nuts out of the battalion. Because the chief's old lady must have had mighty hot pants to judge by the size of his you know. We still get rumours from the orderly room: they correspond. Seems there was more to it than sex. You never know the whole story. And the very same Mahlke – I was there – smoked out a partisan ammunition dump single-handed near Gross-Bislaw. It's a wild story. A plain ordinary pond like a whole lot around here. We were out there partly for work, partly for field training. We'd been lying beside this pond for half an hour, and Mahlke keeps looking and looking, and finally he says: Wait a minute, there's something fishy down there. The platoon leader, can't remember his name, grinned, so did we, but he said to go ahead. Before you could say boo, Mahlke has his clothes off and dives into the muck. And what do you know: the fourth time under, but not two feet below the surface, he finds the entrance to an ultra-modern ammunition dump with a hydraulic loading system. All we had to do was carry the stuff away, four truckloads, and the chief had to commend him in front of the whole battalion. In spite of the business with his old lady, they say he even put him in for a medal. He was in the army when it came, but they sent it on. He was going into the tanks if they took him.'

I restrained myself at first. The same with Winter, Jürgen Kupka and Bansemer; we all shut up when the conversation came around to Mahlke. When we chanced to pass Officers' Row – on hikes or on our way to the supply room – we would exchange furtive smiles of con-nivance, for the second house on the left still had no rabbit hutch. Or a meaningful glance would pass between us because a cat lurked motionless in the gently waving grass. We became a kind of secret clan, though I wasn't very fond of Winter and Kupka, and still less of Bansemer.

Four weeks before the end of our stint, the rumours began to creep in. Partisans had been active in the region; we were on twenty-four-hour alert, never out of our clothes, though we never caught anybody and we ourselves suffered no losses. The same room orderly who had issued Mahlke his uniform and taken him to be deloused, brought the news from the office: 'In the first place there's a letter from Mahlke to the former commander's wife. It's being forwarded to France. In the second place, there's a letter from up top, full of questions about Mahlke. They're still working on it. I always knew that Mahlke had it in him. But he certainly hasn't let any grass grow under his feet. In the old days you had to be an officer if you wanted something nice to wrap around your neck, no matter how badly it ached. Nowadays every private gets his chance. He must be just about the youngest. Lord, when I think of him with those ears . . . '

At that point words began to roll out of my mouth.

Then Winter spoke up. And Jürgen Kupka and Bansemer had their own bit to chip in.

'Oh, Mahlke. We've known him for years.'

'We had him in school.'

'He had a weakness for neck wear when he was only fourteen.'

'Christ, yes. Remember when he swiped that lieutenant commander's thingamajig off the hook in gym class. Here's how it . . . '

'Naw, you gotta begin with the gramophone.'

'What about the tinned food? I suppose that was nothing. Right in the beginning he always wore a screwdriver . . . '

'Wait a minute! If you want to begin at the beginning, you'll have to go back to the Schlagball match in Heinrich-Ehlers field. Here's how it was: We're lying on the ground and Mahlke's asleep. So a grey cat comes creeping across the field, heading straight for Mahlke. And when the cat sees that neck bobbing up and down, she says to herself, my word, that's a mouse. And she jumps . . . '

'That's a load of balls. Pilenz picked up the cat and put it . . . You can't tell me anything different.'

Two days later we had official confirmation. It was announced at morning roll call: A former Labour Service man from Tuchel-North battalion, serving first as a simple machine-gunner, then as a sergeant and tank commander, always in the thick of battle, strategically important position, so and so many Russian tanks, and furthermore, etcetera etcetera.

Our replacements were expected and we were beginning to turn in our rags when I received a clipping that my mother had cut out of the *Vorposten*. There it was printed in black and white: A son of our city, always in the thick of battle, first as a simple machine-gunner, later as a tank commander, and so on and so on.

Chapter Twelve

Marl, sand, glittering bogs, bushes, slanting groups of pines, ponds, hand grenades, carp, clouds over birches, partisans behind the broom, juniper juniper (good old Löns, the naturalist, had come from around there), the cinema in Tuchel – all were left behind. I took nothing with me but my cardboard suitcase and a little bunch of tired heather. Even during the trip I began irrationally but stubbornly to look for Mahlke, while throwing the heather between the lines after Karthaus, in every suburban station and finally in Central Station, outside the ticket windows, in the crowds of soldiers who had poured out of the furlough trains, in the doorway of the control office, and in the train to Langfuhr. I felt ridiculous in my outgrown civilian-schoolboy clothes and convinced that everyone could read my mind. I didn't go home – what had I to hope for at home? – but got out near our school, at the Sports Palace stop.

I left my suitcase with the caretaker, but asked him no questions. Sure of what to expect, I raced up the big granite stairway, taking three or more steps at a time. Not that I expected to catch him in the auditorium – both doors stood open, but inside there were only cleaning women, upending the benches and scrubbing them – for whom? I turned off to the left: squat granite pillars good for cooling feverish foreheads. The marble memorial tablet for the dead of both wars: still quite a lot of room to spare. Lessing in his niche. Classes were in session, for the corridors were empty, except for one spindle-legged Fourth Former carrying a rolled map through the all-pervading octagonal stench. 3a – 3b – art room – 5a – glass case for stuffed mammals – what was in it now? A cat of

111

course. But where was the delirious mouse? Past the conference room. And there at the end of the corridor, with the bright front window at his back, between the secretariat and the principal's office, stood the Great Mahlke, mouseless – for from his neck hung that very special article, the abracadabra, the magnet, the exact opposite of an onion, the galvanized four-leaf clover, good old Schinkel's brain child, the trinket, the all-day sucker, the thingamajig, the Iwillnotutterit.

And the mouse? It was asleep, hibernating in June. Slumbering beneath a heavy blanket, for Mahlke had put on weight. Not that anyone, fate or an author, had erased or obliterated it, as Racine obliterated the rat from his escutcheon, tolerating only the swan. Mahlke's heraldic animal was still the mouse, which acted up in its dreams when Mahlke swallowed; for from time to time the Great Mahlke, notwithstanding his glorious decoration, had to swallow.

How did he look? I have said that he had filled out in action, not too much, about two thicknesses of blotting paper. You were half leaning, half sitting on the white enamelled window sill. You were wearing the bandit-like combination of black and field-grey, common to all those who served in the Tank Corps: grey-bloused trousers concealed the shafts of black, highly polished combat boots. The black, tight-fitting tank crew jacket bunched up under the arms, making them stand out like handles, but it was becoming even so and made you look frail in spite of the few pounds you had gained. No decorations on the jacket. And yet you had both Crosses and some other thing, but no wound insignia: the Virgin had made you invulnerable. It was perfectly understandable that there should be nothing on the chest to distract attention from the new eye-catcher. Around your waist a worn and negligently polished pistol belt, and below it only a hand's breadth of goods, for the tank jacket was very short, which

112

is why it was sometimes called a monkey-jacket. Sagging from the weight of the pistol, which hung down nearly to your arse, the belt relieved the stiffness of your attitude and gave you a lopsided, jaunty look. But your grey field cap sat straight and severe without the then as now customary tilt; a rectilinear crease down the middle recalled your old love of symmetry and the parting that divided your hair in your schoolboy and diving days, when you planned, or so you said, to become a clown. Nevertheless, the redeemer's hair-do was gone. Even before curing your chronic throat trouble with a piece of metal, they must have given you the ludicrous brush cut which was then characteristic of recruits and today gives some of our pipe-smoking intellectuals their air of functional asceticism. But the countenance was still that of a redeemer: the eagle on your inflexibly vertical cap spread its wings over your brow like the dove of the Holy Ghost. Thin skin, sensitive to the light. Blackheads on fleshy nose. Lowered eyelids traversed by fine red veins. And when I stood breathless between you and the stuffed cat, your eyes scarcely widened.

A little joke: 'Greetings, Sergeant Mahlke!' My joke fell flat. 'I'm waiting for Klohse. He's giving a maths class somewhere.'

'He'll be very pleased.'

'I want to speak to him about the lecture.'

'Have you been in the auditorium?'

'My lecture's ready, every word of it.'

'Have you seen the cleaning women? They're scrubbing down the benches.'

'I'll look in later with Klohse. We'll have to discuss the seating arrangement on the platform.'

'He'll be very pleased.'

'I'm going to suggest that they limit the audience to students from the lower third up.'

'Does Klohse know you're waiting?'

'Miss Hersching from the secretariat has gone in to tell him.'

'Well, he'll be very pleased.'

'My lecture will be short but full of action.'

'I should think so. Good Lord, man, how did you swing it so quick?'

'Have a little patience, my dear Pilenz: all the circumstances will be discussed in my lecture.'

'My, won't Klohse be pleased!'

'I'm going to ask him not to introduce me.'

'Mallenbrandt maybe?'

'The proctor can announce the lecture. That's enough.'

'Well, he'll be very . . . '

The bell signal leapt from floor to floor, announcing that classes were at an end. Only then did Mahlke open both eyes wide. Short, sparse lashes. His bearing was meant to be free and easy, but he was tensed to leap. Disturbed by something behind my back, I turned half toward the glass case: the cat wasn't grey, more on the black side. It crept unerringly toward us, disclosing a white bib. Stuffed cats are able to creep more convincingly than live ones. 'The Domestic Cat', said a calligraphed cardboard sign. The bell stopped, an aggressive stillness set in; the mouse woke up and the cat took on more and more meaning. Consequently I cracked a little joke and another little joke in the direction of the window; I said something about his mother and his aunt; I talked, in order to give him courage, about his father, his father's locomotive, his father's death near Dirschau, and his father's posthumous award for bravery: 'How happy your father would be if he were still alive!'

But before I had finished conjuring up Mahlke's father and persuading the mouse that there was no need to fear the cat, Dr Waldemar Klohse, our principal, stepped between us with his high, smooth voice. Klohse uttered no congratulations, he didn't address Mahlke as Sergeant or Bearer of the Thingamajig, nor did he say, Mr Mahlke, I am sincerely pleased. After evincing a pointed interest in my experience in the Labour Service and in the natural beauties of Tuchler Heath – 'you will remember that Löns grew up there' – he sent a trim column of words marching over Mahlke's field cap: 'So you see, Mahlke, you've made it after all. Have you been to the Horst-Wessel School? My esteemed colleague, Dr Wendt, will certainly be glad to see you. I feel sure that you will wish to deliver a little lecture for the benefit of your former schoolmates, to reinforce their confidence in our armed forces. Would you please step into my office for a moment?'

And the Great Mahlke, his arms raised like handles, followed Dr Klohse into the principal's office and in the doorway whisked his cap off his stubblehead. Oh that bumpy dome! A schoolboy in uniform on his way to a solemn conference, the outcome of which I did not wait for, although I was curious to know what the already wide-awake and enterprising mouse would say, after the interview, to that cat which though stuffed had never ceased to creep.

Nasty little triumph! Once again I enjoyed my moment of superiority. Just wait and see! He can't won't can't give in. I'll help him. I'll speak to Klohse. I'll find words to touch his heart. Too bad they've taken Papa Brunies to Stutthof. He'd come out with his good old Eichendorff in his pocket and extend a helping hand.

But no one could help Mahlke. Perhaps if I had spoken to Klohse. But I did speak to him; for half an hour I let him blow peppermint breath in my face. I was crushed, and my answer was very feeble: 'By all reasonable standards, Sir, you are probably right. But couldn't you in view of, I mean, in this particular case? On the one hand, I understand you perfectly. Yes, it can't be denied, a school has to have discipline. What's done can't be

115

undone, but on the other hand, and because he was so young when he lost his father . . . '

And I spoke to Father Gusewski, and to Tulla, whom I asked to speak to Störtebeker and his gang. I went to see my former group leader in the Young Folk. He had a wooden leg from Crete and was sitting behind a desk in the section headquarters on Winterplatz. He was delighted with my proposal and cursed all schoolmasters: 'Of course, we'll do it. Bring him over. I dimly remember him. Wasn't there some sort of trouble? Forget it. I'll drum up the biggest crowd I can. Even the League of German Girls and the Women's Association. I can get a hall across from the postal administration, seats three hundred and fifty . . . '

Father Gusewski wanted to gather his old ladies and a dozen Catholic workers in the sacristy, for the public meeting halls were not available to him.

'Perhaps, to bring his talk into line with the concerns of the Church,' Father Gusewski suggested, 'your friend could say something about St George to begin with and conclude with a word or two about the power of prayer in times of great distress.' He was eagerly looking forward to the lecture.

The young delinquents associated with Störtebeker and Tulla Pokriefke thought they had a cellar that would fill the bill. A youngster by the name of Rennwand, whom I knew slightly – he served as an altar boy in the Church of the Sacred Heart – spoke of the place in the most mysterious terms: Mahlke would need a safe-conduct and would have to surrender his pistol. 'Of course we'll have to blindfold him on the way. And he'll have to sign a pledge not to tell a living soul, but that's a mere formality. Of course we'll pay well, either in cash or in Army watches. We don't do anything for nothing and we don't expect him to.'

But Mahlke accepted none of these possibilities, and

he was not interested in pay. I tried to prod him: 'What do you want anyway? Nothing's good enough for you. Why don't you go out to Tuchel-North. There's a new batch of recruits. The room orderly and the cook remember you. I'm sure they'd be pleased as punch to have you make a speech.'

Mahlke listened calmly to all my suggestions, smiling in places, nodded assent, asked practical questions about organizing the meeting in question, and once the obstacles were disposed of, tersely and morosely rejected every single proposition, even an invitation from the regional party headquarters, for from the start he had but one aim in mind: the auditorium of our school. He wanted to stand in the dust-swarming light that trickled through neo-Gothic ogival windows. He wanted to address the stench of three hundred schoolboys, farting high and farting low. He wanted the whetted scalps of his former teachers around him and behind him. He wanted to face the oil painting at the end of the auditorium, showing Baron von Conradi, founder of the school, caseous and immortal beneath heavy varnish. He wanted to enter the auditorium through one of the old-brown folding doors and after a brief, perhaps pointed speech, to leave through the other; but Klohse, in knickerbockers with a small check, stood barring both doors at once: 'As a soldier, Mahlke, you ought to realize. No, the cleaning women were scrubbing the benches for no particular reason, not for you, not for your lecture. Your plan may have been excellently conceived, but it cannot be executed. Remember this, Mahlke: There are many mortals who love expensive carpets but are condemned to die on plain floorboards. You must learn renunciation, Mahlke.'

Klohse compromised just a little. He called a meeting of the faculties of both schools, which decided that 'Disciplinary considerations make it imperative . . .'

And the Board of Education confirmed Klohse's report

117

to the effect that a former student, whose past history, even though he, but particularly in view of the troubled and momentous times, though without wishing to exaggerate the importance of an offence which, it must be admitted, was none too recent, nevertheless and because the case is unique of its kind, the faculty of both schools has agreed that . . .

And Klohse wrote a purely personal letter. And Mahlke read that Klohse was not free to act as his heart desired. Unfortunately the times and circumstances were such that an experienced schoolmaster, conscious of his professional responsibilities, could not follow the simple, paternal dictates of his heart; in the interests of the school, he must request manly cooperation in conformity to the old Conradinian spirit; he would gladly attend the lecture which Mahlke, soon, he hoped, and without bitterness, would deliver at the Horst-Wessel School; unless he preferred, like a true hero, to choose the better part of speech and remain silent.

But the Great Mahlke had started down a path resembling that tunnel-like, overgrown, thorny and birdless path in Oliva Castle Park, which had no forks or byways but was nonetheless a labyrinth. In the daytime he slept, played backgammon with his aunt, or sat listless and inactive, apparently waiting for his furlough to be over. But at night he crept with me – I behind him, never ahead of him, seldom by his side – through the Langfuhr night. Our wanderings were not aimless: we concentrated on Baumbachallee, a quiet, genteel, conscientiously blacked-out lane, where nightingales sang and Dr Klohse lived. I weary behind his uniformed back: 'Don't be an ass. You can see it's impossible. And what difference does it make? The few days' leave you've got left. Good Lord, man, don't be an ass. . . . '

But the Great Mahlke wasn't interested in my tedious appeals to reason. He had a different melody in his pro-

118

tuberant ears. Until two in the morning we besieged Baumbachallee and its two nightingales. Twice he was not alone, and we had to let him pass. But when after four nights of vigilance, at about eleven o'clock, Dr Klohse turned in from Schwarzer Weg alone, tall and thin in knickerbockers but without hat or coat, for the air was balmy, and came striding up Baumbachallee, the Great Mahlke's left hand shot out and seized Klohse's shirt collar with its civilian tie. He pushed the school-master against the forged iron fence, behind which bloomed roses whose fragrance – because it was so dark – was overpowering, louder even than the voices of the nightingales. And taking the advice Klohse had given him in his letter, Mahlke chose the better part of speech, heroic silence; without a word he struck the school principal's smooth-shaven face left right with the back and palm of his hand. Both men stiff and formal. Only the sound of the slaps alive and eloquent; for Klohse too kept his small mouth closed, not wishing to mix pepper-mint breath with the scent of roses.

That happened on a Thursday and took less than a minute. We left Klohse standing by the iron fence. That is to say, Mahlke about-faced and strode in his combat boots across the gravel-strewn path beneath the red maple tree, which was not red at night but formed a black screen between us and the sky. I tried to give Klohse something resembling an apology, for Mahlke – and for myself. The slapped man waved me away; he no longer looked slapped but stood stiff as a ramrod, his dark silhouette sustained by roses and the voices of rare birds, embodying the school, its founder, the Conradinian spirit, the Conradinum; for that was the name of our school.

After that we raced through lifeless suburban streets, and from that moment on neither of us had a word to spare for Klohse. Mahlke talked and talked, with exaggerated coolness of problems that seemed to trouble him at that age – and myself, too, to some extent. Such as: Is there a life after death? Or: Do you believe in transmigration? 'I've been reading quite a bit of Kierkegaard lately,' he informed me. And 'you must be sure to read Dostoyevsky. Later, when you're in Russia. It will help you to understand all sorts of things, the mentality and so on.'

Several times we stood on bridges across the Striessbach, a rivulet full of horse leeches. It was pleasant to lean over the railing and wait for rats. Each bridge made the conversation shift from schoolboy banalities – erudition, for instance, about the armour plate, firepower and speed of the world's battleships – to religion and the so-called last questions. On the little Neuschottland bridge we gazed for a long while at the star-studded June sky and then – each for himself – into the stream. Mahlke in an undertone, while below us the shallow outlet of Aktien Pond, carrying away the yeasty vapours of Aktien Brewery, broke over shoals of tin cans: 'Of course I don't believe in God. He's just a swindle to stultify the people. The only thing I believe in is the Virgin Mary. That's why I'm never going to get married.'

There was a sentence succinct and insane enough to be spoken on a bridge. It has stayed with me. Whenever a brook or canal is spanned by a small bridge, whenever there is a gurgling down below and water breaking against the rubbish which disorderly people the world over throw from bridges into rivulets and canals, Mahlke stands beside me in combat boots and tanker's monkey-jacket, leaning over the rail so that the big thingamajig on his neck hangs down vertical, a solemn clown triumphing over cat and mouse with his irrefutable faith: 'Of course not in God. A swindle to stultify the people. There's only Mary. I'll never get married.'

And he uttered a good many more words which fell

120

into the Striessbach. Possibly we circled Max-Halbe-Platz ten times, raced twelve times up and down Heeres-anger. Stood undecided at the terminus of Line No. 5. Looked on, not without hunger, as the tram conductors and marcelled conductresses, sitting in the blued-out trailer, bit into sandwiches and drank out of thermos bottles.

... and then came a tram – or should have – in which the conductoress under the cocked cap was Tulla Pokriefke, who had been drafted as a wartime helper several weeks before. We'd have spoken to her and I would certainly have made a date with her if she had been working on Line No. 5. But as it was, we saw only her little profile behind the dark-blue glass and we were not sure.

I said: 'You ought to give it a try with her.'

Mahlke, tormented: 'I just told you that I'm never going to get married.'

I: 'It would cheer you up.'

He: 'And who's going to cheer me up afterwards?'

I tried to joke: 'The Virgin Mary of course.'

He had misgivings: 'What if she's offended?'

I offered my help. 'If you want me to, I'll be Gusewski's altar boy tomorrow morning.'

I was amazed at the alacrity with which he said: 'It's a deal!' And he went off toward the trailer which still held out the promise of Tulla Pokriefke's profile in a conductor's cap. Before he got in, I called out: 'Say, how much more leave have you got left?'

And from the door of the trailer the Great Mahlke said: 'My train left four and a half hours ago. If nothing has gone wrong, it must be pulling into Modlin.'

Chapter Thirteen

'*Misereatur vestri omnipotens Deus, et, dismissis peccatis vestris* . . . ' The words issued light as a soap bubble from Father Gusewski's pursed lips, glittered in all the colours of the rainbow, swayed hesitantly, broke loose from the hidden reed, and rose at last, mirroring windows, the altar, the Virgin, mirroring you, me, everything – and burst painlessly, struck by the bubbles of the absolution. '*Indulgentiam, absolutionem et remissionem peccatorum vestrorum* . . . ' and the moment these new bubbles of spirit were pricked in their turn by the Amen of the seven or eight faithful, Gusewski elevated the Host and began with full-rounded lips to blow the big bubble, the bubble of bubbles. For a moment it trembled terror-stricken in the draught; then with the bright-red tip of his tongue, he sent it aloft; and it rose and rose until at length it fell and passed away, close to the second pew facing the altar of the Virgin: '*Ecce Agnus Dei* . . . '

Of those taking communion, Mahlke was first to kneel. He knelt before the 'LordIamnotworthythatthoushouldst enterundermyroof' had been repeated three times. Even before I steered Gusewski down the altar steps to the communicants' rail, he leaned his head back, so that his face, peaked after a sleepless night, lay parallel to the whitewashed concrete ceiling, and parted his lips with his tongue. A moment's wait, while over his head the priest makes a small quick sign of the Cross with the wafer intended for this communicant. Sweat oozed from Mahlke's pores and formed glistening beads which quickly broke, punctured by his beard stubble. His eyes stood out as though boiled. Possibly the blackness of his tank jacket enhanced the pallor of his face. Despite the woolliness of

122

his tongue, he did not swallow. In humble self-effacement the iron object that had rewarded his childish scribbling and crossing-out of so and so many Russian tanks crossed itself and lay motionless over his top collar button. It was only when Father Gusewski laid the host of Mahlke's tongue and Mahlke partook of the light pastry, that you swallowed; and then the thingamajig joined in.

Let us all three celebrate the sacrament, once more and forever: You kneel, I stand behind dry skin. Sweat distends your pores. The reverend father deposits the Host on your coated tongue. All three of us have just ended on the same syllable, whereupon a mechanism pulls your tongue back in. Lips stick together. Propagation of sobs, the big thingamajig trembles, and I know that the Great Mahlke will leave St Mary's Chapel fortified, his sweat will dry; if immediately afterwards drops of moisture glistened on his face, they were raindrops. It was drizzling.

In the dry sacristy Gusewski said: 'He must be waiting outside. Maybe we should call him in, but . . .

I said: 'Don't worry, father. I'll take care of him.'

Gusewski, his hands busy with the sachets of lavender in the closet: 'You don't think he'll do anything rash?'

For once I made no move to help him out of his vestments: 'You'd better keep out of it, Father.' But to Mahlke when he stood before me wet in his uniform, I said: 'You damn fool, what are you hanging around here for? Get down to the assembly point on Hochstriess. Tell them some story about missing your train. I refuse to have anything to do with it.'

With those words I should have left him, but I stayed and got wet. Rain is a binder. I tried to reason with him: 'They won't bite your head off if you're quick about it. Tell them something was wrong with your mother or your aunt.'

Mahlke nodded when I made a point, let his lower jaw sag from time to time, and laughed for no reason. Then suddenly he bubbled over: 'It was wonderful last night with the Pokriefke kid. I wouldn't have thought it. She's not the way she puts on. All right, I'll tell you the honest truth: It's because of her that I don't want to go back. Seems to me that I've done my bit – wouldn't you say so? I'm going to put in a petition. They can ship me out to Gross-Boschpol as an instructor. Let other people be brave. It's not that I'm scared, I've just had enough. Can you understand that?'

I refused to fall for his nonsense; I pinned him down. 'Oho, so it's on account of the Pokriefke kid. Hell, that wasn't her. She works on the No. 2 line to Oliva, not on the No. 5. Everybody knows that. You're scared shitless, that's all. I can see how you feel.'

He was determined that there should be something between them. 'You can take my word for it about Tulla. The fact is she took me home with her, lives on Elsenstrasse. Her mother doesn't mind – But you're right, I've had my belly full. Maybe I'm scared too. I was scared before Mass. It's better now.'

'I thought you didn't believe in God and all that stuff.'

'That's got nothing to do with it.'

'OK, forget it. And now what?'

'Maybe Störtebeker and the boys could ... You know them pretty well, don't you?'

'Nothing doing. I'm having no further dealings with those characters. It's not healthy. You should have asked the Pokriefke kid in case you really ... '

'Don't be stupid. I can't show my face on Osterzeile. If they're not there already, it won't be long – say, could I hide in your cellar, just for a few days?'

That too struck me as unhealthy. 'You've got other places to hide. What about your relatives in the country? Or in Tulla's uncle's woodshed. .... Or on the barge.'

For a while the word hung in mid-air. 'In this filthy weather?' Mahlke said. But the thing was already decided;

124

and though I refused stubbornly and prolixly to go with him, though I too spoke of the filthy weather, it gradually became apparent that I would have to go: rain is a binder.

We spent a good hour tramping from Neuschottland to Schellmühl and back, and then down the endless Posedowskiweg. We took shelter in the lee of at least two advertising pillars, bearing always the same posters warning the public against those sinister and unpatriotic figures Coalthief and Spendthrift, and then we resumed our tramp. From the main entrance of the Women's Hospital we saw the familiar backdrop: behind the railroad embankment, the gable-roof and spire of the sturdy old Conradinum; but he wasn't looking or he saw something else. Then we stood for half an hour in the shelter of the Reichskolonie tram stop, under the echoing tin roof with three or four grade-school boys. At first they spent the time rough-housing and pushing each other off the bench. Mahlke had his back turned to them, but it didn't help. Two of them came up with open copybooks and said something in broad dialect. 'Aren't you supposed to be in school?' I asked.

'Not until nine. If we decide to go.'

'Well, hand them over, but make it fast.'

Mahlke wrote his name and rank in the upper left-hand corner of the last page of both copybooks. They were not satisfied, they wanted the exact number of tanks he had knocked out – and Mahlke gave in; as though filling in a money order blank, he wrote the numbers first in figures, then in letters. Then he had to write his piece in two more copybooks. I was about to take back my fountain pen when one of the kids asked: 'Where'd you knock 'em off, in Bjälgerott (Byelgorod) or Schietemier (Zhitomir)?'

Mahlke ought just to have nodded and they would have subsided. But he whispered in a hoarse voice: 'No, most of them around Kovel, Brody and Brzezany. And in

125

April when we knocked out the First Armoured Corps at Buczacz.'

The youngsters wanted it all in writing and again I had to unscrew the fountain pen. They called two more of their contemporaries in out of the rain. It was always the same back that held still for the others to write on. He wanted to stretch, he would have liked to hold out his own copybook; they wouldn't let him: there's always one stooge. Mahlke had to write Kovel and Brody-Brzezany, Cerkassy and Buczacz. His hand shook more and more, and again the sweat oozed from his pores. Questions spurted from their grubby faces: 'Was ya in Kriewäurock (Krivoi Rog) too?' Every mouth open. In every mouth teeth missing. Paternal grandfather's eyes. Ears from the mother's side. And each one had nostrils: 'And where'd ya think they'll send ya next?'

'He ain't allowed to tell. What's the use of asking?'

'I bet he's gonna be in the invasion.'

'They're keepin' 'im for after the war.'

'Ask him if he's been at the Führer's HQ?'

'How about it, Uncle?'

'Can't you see he's a sergeant?'

'You gotta picture?'

"Cause we collect 'em.'

'How much more leave ya got?'

'Yeah, whenner ya leavin?'

'Ya still be here tomorrow?'

'Yeah, when's yer time up?'

Mahlke fought his way out, stumbling over satchels. My fountain pen stayed in the shelter. Marathon through crosshatching. Side by side through puddles: rain is a binder. It was only after we passed the stadium that the boys fell back. But still they shouted after us; they had no intention of going to school. To this day they want to return my fountain pen.

When we reached the kitchen gardens outside Neuschottland, we stopped to catch our breath. I had a rage inside me and my rage was getting kittens. I thrust an accusing forefinger at the accursed thingamajig and Mahlke quickly removed it from his neck. Like the screwdriver years before, it was attached to a shoelace. Mahlke wanted to give it to me, but I shook my head. 'Hell, no, but thanks for nothing.'

But he didn't toss the scrap metal into the wet bushes; he had a back pocket.

How am I going to get out of here? The gooseberries behind the makeshift fences were unripe: Mahlke began to pick with both hands. My pretext cast about for words. He gobbled and spat out skins. 'Wait for me here, I'll be back in half an hour. You've got to have something to eat or you won't last long on the barge.'

If Mahlke had said 'Be sure you come back,' I would have lit out for good. He scarcely nodded as I left; with all ten fingers he was reaching through the fence laths at the bushes; his mouth full of berries, he compelled loyalty: rain is a binder.

Mahlke's aunt opened the door. Good that his mother wasn't home. I could have taken some edibles from our house, but I thought: what's he got his family for? Besides, I was curious about his aunt. I was disappointed. She stood there in her kitchen apron and asked no questions. Through open doors came the smell of something that makes teeth squeak: rhubarb was being cooked at the Mahlkes'.

'We're giving a little party for Joachim. We've got plenty of stuff to drink, but in case we get hungry . . . . '

Without a word she went to the kitchen and came back with two two-pound cans of pork. She also had a can opener, but it wasn't the same one that Mahlke had brought up from the barge when he found the canned frogs' legs in the galley. While she was out wondering what to give me – the Mahlkes always had their cupboards full, relatives in the country – I stood restless in the hallway, gazing at the photograph of Mahlke's father and Fireman Labuda. The locomotive had no steam up.

The aunt came back with a shopping net and some newspaper to wrap the cans in. 'Before you eat the pork,' she said, 'you'll have to warm it up some. If you don't it'll be too heavy; it'll sit on your stomach.'

If I asked before leaving whether anyone had been around asking for Joachim, the answer was no. But I didn't ask, I just turned around in the doorway and said: 'Joachim sends you his love,' though Mahlke hadn't sent anything at all, not even to his mother.

He wasn't curious either when I reappeared between the gardens in the same rain, hung the net on a fence lath, and stood rubbing my strangled fingers. He was still gobbling unripe gooseberries, compelling me, like his aunt, to worry about his physical well-being: 'You're going to upset your stomach. Let's get going.' But even then he stripped three handfuls from the dripping branches and filled his trouser pockets. As we looped around Neuschottland and the housing development between Wolfsweg and Bärenweg, he was still spitting out hard gooseberry skins. As we stood on the rear platform of the streetcar trailer and the rainy air field passed by to the left of us, he was still pouring them in.

He was getting on my nerves with his gooseberries. Besides, the rain was letting up. The grey turned milky: made me feel like getting out and leaving him alone with his gooseberries. But I only said: 'They've already come asking about you. Two plain clothes men.'

'Really?' He spat out the skins on the platform floor. 'What about my mother? Does she know?'

'Your mother wasn't there. Only your aunt.'

'Must have been shopping.'

'I doubt it.'

'Then she was over at Schielkes' helping with the ironing.'

'I'm sorry to say she wasn't there either.'

'Like some gooseberries?'

'She's been taken down to the military district. I wasn't going to tell you.'

We were almost in Brösen before Mahlke ran out of gooseberries. But as we crossed the beach in which the rain had cut its pattern, he was still searching his sopping pockets for more. And when the Great Mahlke heard the sea slapping against the beach and his eyes saw the Baltic, the barge as a far-off backdrop, and the shadows of a few ships in the roadstead, he said: 'I can't swim.' Though I had already taken off my shoes and trousers. The horizon drew a line through both his pupils.

'Is this a time to make jokes?'

'No kidding. I've got a belly-ache. Damn gooseberries.'

At this I swore and looked through my pockets and swore some more and found a mark and a little change. I ran to Brösen and rented a boat for two hours from old man Kreft. It wasn't as easy as it looks on paper, though Kreft didn't ask very many questions and helped me to launch the boat. When I pulled up on the beach, Mahlke lay writhing in the sand, uniform and all. I had to kick him to make him get up. He shivered, sweated, dug both fists into the pit of his stomach; but even today I can't make myself believe in that belly-ache in spite of unripe gooseberries on an empty stomach.

'Why don't you go behind the dunes? Go ahead. On the double!' He walked hunched over, making curved tracks, and disappeared behind the beach grass. Maybe I could have seen his cap, but though nothing was moving in or out, I kept my eyes on the breakwater. When he came back, he was still hunched over but he helped me to shove

129

off. I sat him down in the stern, stowed the net with the cans in it on his knees, and put the wrapped can opener in his hands. When the water darkened behind the second sandbank, I said: 'Now *you* can take a few strokes.'

The Great Mahlke didn't even shake his head; he sat doubled up, clutching the wrapped can opener and looking through me; for we were sitting face to face.

Although I have never again to this day set foot in a rowing boat, we are still sitting face to face: and his fingers are fidgeting. His neck is bare, but his cap straight. Sand trickling from the folds in his uniform. No rain, but forehead dripping. Every muscle tense. Eyes popping out of his head. With whom has he exchanged noses? Both knees wobbling. No cat off shore. But the mouse scurrying.

Yet it wasn't cold. Only when the clouds parted and the sun burst through the seams did spots of gooseflesh pass over the scarcely breathing surface of the water and assail our boat. 'Take a few strokes, it'll warm you up.' The answer was a chattering of teeth from the stern. And from intermittent groans chopped words were born into the world: ' . . . fat lot of good it did me. Might have guessed. Fuss for a lot of nonsense. Too bad. It would have been a good lecture. Would have started in with explanations, the sights, armour-piercing shells, Maybach engines, and so on. When I was a loader, I had to come up all the time to tighten up bolts, even under fire. But I wasn't going to talk about myself the whole time. My father and Labuda, the fireman. A few words about the accident by Dirschau. How my father by his courage and self-sacrifice. The way I always thought of my father as I sat there at the sights. Hadn't even received the sacraments when he. Thanks for the candles that time. O thou most pure. Mother inviolate. Through whose intercession partake. Most amiable. Full of grace. It's the honest truth. My first battle north of Kursk proved it. And in the tangle outside Orel when they counter-attacked. And in August by the Vorskla the way

130

the Mother of God. They all laughed and put the division chaplain on my tail. Sure, but then we stabilized the front. Unfortunately, I was transferred to Centre Sector, or they wouldn't have broken through so quick at Kharkov. She appeared to me again near Korosten when the 59th Corps. She never had the child, it was always the picture she was holding. Yes, Dr Klohse, it's hanging in our hall beside the brushbag. And she didn't hold it over her breast, no, lower down. I had the locomotive in my sights, plain as day. Just had to hold steady between my father and Labuda. Four hundred. Direct hit. Did you see, Pilenz, I always aim between turret and boiler. Gives them a good airing. No, Dr Klohse, she didn't speak. But to tell you the honest truth, she doesn't have to speak to me. Proofs? She held the picture, I tell you. Or in mathematics. Suppose you're teaching maths. You assume that parallel lines meet at infinity. You'll admit that adds up to something like transcendence. That's how it was that time in the second line east of Kazan. It was the third day of Christmas. She came in from the left and headed for a clump of woods at convoy speed, twenty miles an hour. Just had to keep her in my sights. Hey, Pilenz, two strokes on the left, we're missing the barge.'

At first Mahlke's outline of his lecture was little more than a chattering of teeth, but then he had them under control. Through it all he kept an eye on our course. The rhythm at which he spoke made me row so fast that the sweat poured from my forehead, while his pores dried and called it a day. Not for a single stroke was I sure whether or not he saw anything more over the expanding bridge than the customary gulls.

Before we hove alongside, he sat relaxed in the stern playing negligently with the can opener that he had taken out of its paper. He no longer complained of belly-ache. He stood before me on the barge, and when I had tied up, his hands busied themselves on his neck: the big thingamajig from his rear pocket was in place again. Rubbed his hands, the sun broke through, stretched his legs: Mahlke paced the deck as though taking possession, hummed a snatch of litany, waved up at the gulls, and played the cheery uncle who turns up for a visit after years of adventurous absence, bringing himself as a present. O happy reunion! 'Hello, boys and girls, you haven't changed a bit!'

I found it hard to join in the game: 'Get a move on. Old man Kreft only gave me the boat for an hour and a half. At first he said only an hour.'

Mahlke calmed down: 'OK, never detain a busy man. I say, look at that bucket, the one next to the tanker, she's lying pretty low. I'll bet she's a Swede. Just for your information, we're going to row out there as soon as it gets dark. I want you back here at nine o'clock. I've a right to ask that much of you – or haven't I?'

The visibility was poor and of course it was imposstble to make out the nationality of the freighter in the road-stead. Mahlke began to undress elaborately, meanwhile spouting a lot of incoherent nonsense. A few words about Tulla Pokriefke: 'A hot number, take it from me.' Gossip about Father Gusewski. 'They say he sold goods on the black market. Altar cloths too. Or rather the coupons for the stuff.' A couple of funny stories about his aunt: 'But you've got to give her credit for one thing, she always got along with my father, even when they were both kids in the country.' More about the locomotive: 'Look, you might drop back to our house and get the picture, with or without the frame. No, better let it go. Just weigh me down.'

He stood there in red gym pants, a vestige of our school tradition. He had carefully folded his uniform into the regulation bundle and stowed it away in his old-accus-tomed place behind the pilot house. His boots looked like bedtime. 'You got everything?' I asked. 'Don't forget the opener.' He shifted the medal from left to right and

132

chattered schoolboy nonsense as if he hadn't a care in the world: 'Tonnage of the Argentine battleship *Moreno*? Speed in knots? How much armour plate at the waterline? Year built? When remodelled? How many 150-millimetre guns on the *Vittorio Veneto*?'

I answered sluggishly, but I was pleased to find that I still knew the answers. 'Are you going to take both cans at once?'

'I'll see.'

'Don't forget the can opener. There it is.'

'You're looking after me like a mother.'

'Well, if I were you, I'd start going downstairs.'

'Right you are. The place must be in a pretty sad state.'

'You're not supposed to spend the winter there.'

'The main thing is I hope the lighter works. There's plenty of fuel.'

'I wouldn't throw that thing away. Maybe you can sell it as a souvenir somewhere. You never can tell.'

Mahlke tossed the object from hand to hand. He slipped off the bridge and started looking step by step for the hatch, holding out his hands like a tightrope walker, though one arm was weighed down by the net with the two cans in it. His knees made bow waves. The sun broke through again for a moment and his backbone and the sinews in his neck cast a shadow to leftward.

'Must be half past ten. Maybe later.'

'It's not as cold as I expected.'

'It's always that way after the rain.'

'My guess is water 65, air 68.'

There was a dredger in the channel, not far from the harbour-mouth buoy. Signs of activity on board, but the sounds were pure imagination, the wind was in the wrong direction. Mahlke's mouse was imaginary too, for even after his groping feet had found the rim of the hatch, he showed me only his back.

133

Over and over the same custom-made question dins into my ears: Did he say anything else before he went down? The only thing I am halfway sure of is that angular glance up at the bridge, over his left shoulder. He crouched down a moment to moisten himself, darkening the flag-red gym pants, and with his right hand improved his grip on the net with the tin cans – but what about the all-day sucker? It wasn't hanging from his neck. Had he thrown it away without my noticing? Where is the fish that will bring it to me? Did he say something more over his shoulder? Up at the gulls? Or toward the beach or the ships in the roadstead? Did he curse all rodents? I don't think I heard you say 'Well, see you tonight.' Head first and weighed down with two cans of pork, he dived: the rounded back and the rear end followed the neck. A white foot kicked into the void. The water over the hatch resumed its usual rippling play.

Then I took my foot off the can opener. The can opener and I remained behind. If only I had got right into the boat, cast off and away: 'Hell, he'll manage without it.' But I stayed, counting the seconds. I let the dredger with its rising and falling chain buckets count for me, and frantically followed its count: thirty-two, thirty-three rusty seconds. Thirty-six, thirty-seven mud-heaving seconds. For forty-one, forty-two badly oiled seconds, forty-seven, forty-eight, forty-nine seconds, the dredger with its rising, falling, dipping buckets did what it could: deepened the Neufahrwasser harbour channel and helped me measure the time: Mahlke, with his cans of pork but no can opener, with or without the black candy whose sweetness had bitterness for a twin, must by then have moved into the erstwhile radio shack of the Polish mine sweeper *Rybitwa*.

Though we had not arranged for any signals, you might have knocked. Once again and again once again, I let the dredger count thirty seconds for me. By all calculable

134

odds, or whatever the expression is, he must have. . . . The gulls, cutting out patterns between barge and sky were getting on my nerves. But when for no apparent reason the gulls suddenly veered away, the absence of gulls got on my nerves. I began, first with my heels, then with Mahlke's boots, to belabour the deck of the bridge: flakes of rust went flying, crumbs of gull droppings danced at every blow. Can opener in hammering fist, Pilenz shouted: 'Come up! You've forgotten the can opener, the can opener . . . ' Wild, then rhythmic shouting and hammering. Then a pause. Unfortunately I didn't know Morse code. Two-three two-three, I hammered. Shouted myself hoarse: 'Can o-pen-er! Can o-pen-er!'

Ever since that Friday I've known what silence is. Silence sets in when gulls veer away. Nothing can make more silence than a dredger at work when the wind carries away its iron noises. But it was Joachim Mahlke who made the greatest silence of all by not responding to my noise.

So then I rowed back. But before rowing back, I threw the can opener in the direction of the dredger, but didn't hit it.

So then I threw away the can opener and rowed back, returned old man Kreft's boat, had to pay an extra thirty pfennigs, and said: 'Maybe I'll be back again this evening. Maybe I'll want the boat again.'

So then I threw away, rowed back, returned, paid extra, said I'd be, sat down in the tram and rode, as they say, home.

So then I didn't go straight home after all, but rang the door-bell on Osterzeile, I asked no questions, just got them to give me the locomotive and frame, for hadn't I said to Mahlke and to old man Kreft too for that matter: 'Maybe I'll be back again this evening. . . . '

So my mother had just finished making lunch when I

came home with the photograph. One of the heads of the labour police at the railroad car factory was eating with us. There was no fish, and beside my plate there was a letter for me from the military district.

So then I read and read my draft notice. My mother began to cry, which embarrassed the company. 'I won't be leaving until Sunday night,' I said, and then, paying no attention to our visitor: 'Do you know what's become of Papa's binoculars?'

So then, with binoculars and photograph, I rode out to Brösen on Saturday morning, and not that same evening as agreed – the fog would have spoiled the visibility, and it was raining again. I picked out the highest spot on the wooded dunes, in front of the Soldiers' Monument. I stood on the top step of the platform – above me towered the obelisk crowned with its golden ball, sheenless in the rain – and for half if not three quarters of an hour I held the binoculars to my eyes. It was only when everything turned to a blur that I lowered the glasses and looked into the dogrose bushes.

So nothing was moving on the barge. Two empty combat boots were clearly distinguishable. Gulls still hovered over the rust, then gulls settled like powder on deck and shoes. In the roadstead the same ships as the day before. But no Swede among them, no neutral ship of any kind. The dredger had scarcely moved. The weather seemed to be on the mend. Once again I rode, as they say, home. My mother helped me to pack my cardboard suitcase.

So then I packed: I had removed the photograph from the frame and since you hadn't claimed it, packed it at the bottom. On top of your father, on top of Fireman Labuda and your father's locomotive that had no steam up, I piled my underwear, the usual rubbish, and the diary which was lost near Cottbus along with the photograph and my letters.

Who will supply me with a good ending? For what began with cat and mouse torments me today in the form of crested terns on ponds bordered with rushes. Though I avoid nature, educational films show me these clever aquatic birds. Or the newsreels make me watch attempts to raise sunken freight barges in the Rhine or underwater operations in Hamburg harbour: it seems they are blasting the fortifications near the Howald Shipyard and salvaging aerial mines. Men go down with flashing, slightly battered helmets, men rise to the surface. Arms are held out toward them, the helmet is unscrewed, removed: but never does the Great Mahlke light a cigarette on the flickering screen; it's always somebody else who lights up.

When a circus comes to town, it can count on me as a customer. I know them all, or just about; I've spoken with any number of clowns in private, out behind the trailers; but usually they have no sense of humour, and if they've ever heard of a colleague named Mahlke, they won't admit it.

I may as well add that in October 1959 I went to Regensburg to a meeting of those survivors of the war who, like you, had won the Knight's Cross. They wouldn't admit me to the hall. Inside, a Bundeswehr band was playing, or resting between pieces. During one such intermission, I had the lieutenant in charge of the order squad page you from the music platform: 'Sergeant Mahlke is wanted at the entrance.' But you didn't show up. You didn't surface.

Günter Grass
The Rat £3.95

Through the thoughts of a caged female rat we learn the history of the world from the rat perspective, interleaved by Grass's narrator with tales old, new and fantastical of the protagonists of earlier writings. The result is a chilling insight into what the future holds: the human race stands condemned by wasteful consumerism and an urge for self destruction, to be supplanted by its logical successor in the evolutionary chain: the rat.

'Grass has written an apocalyptic novel which goes further than any of his work in plumbing the dangers of our nuclear age; the book is dark, bitter, witty and somehow warming. It asks the obvious fundamental questions — Who controls the world? Who controls the imagination? — but, instead of anguished romanticism, does it with the realism of its own convictions and the convictions of its own imagery'
NEW STATESMAN

'The narrative is seamlessly welded together and lent power by the brown rat that the author has been given for Christmas . . . Reading his prose, as always superbly translated by Ralph Manheim, is like being wakened from the sleep of reason by acid rain' NEW YORK TIMES

'Massive and magnificent' THE DAILY TELEGRAPH

'A magnificently organized howl of anguish'
THE INDEPENDENT

Günter Grass
The Tin Drum £5.95

It was the publication of *The Tin Drum* in 1959 that launched Günter Grass as an author of international repute. Bitter and impassioned, it delivers a scathing dissection of the years from 1925 to 1955 through the eyes of Osker Matzerath, the dwarf whose manic beating on the toy of his retarded childhood fantastically counterpoints the accumulating horrors of Germany and Poland under the Nazis.

'Funny, macabre, disgusting, blasphemous, pathetic, horrifying, emetic, erotic, it is an endless delirium, an outrageous phantasmagoria in which dust from Goethe, Hans Andersen, Swift, Rabelais, Joyce, Aristophanes and Rochester dances on the point of a needle in the flame of a candle that was not worth the game' DAILY TELEGRAPH

'The novel is as monstrous as its hero, pullulating with a kind of anti-life for which one of the most horribly memorable images of the book, a horse's head seething with live eels, serves as a suitable emblem. Günter Grass may have written the nearest thing to a literary masterpiece his generation is capable of producing'
DAVID LODGE, THE SPECTATOR

'This is a big book in every sense, full of extraordinary scenes and characters: even on a single reading it seems prodigally rich in comic invention, and demands to be worried at again and again'
JULIAN MITCHELL, THE SUNDAY TIMES

Dog Years £3.95

First published in 1963, *Dog Years* is perhaps the most violent and unrelenting of Grass's novels. In a fusion of mythology and reality, magic and romance, it charts forty years of German history, commencing from 1917, with the objective of exposing the madness of a society that bred and nurtured the horrors of the Third Reich then anaesthetised itself with the chaos of the resultant disintegration.

'Günter Grass releases, against the grain of history, a troop of obsessional characters, armed often with magical or at least disconcerting powers, who gnaw through the madness of the Third Reich and the chaos of the collapse, into the complacent fabric of modern West Germany' NEAL ASCHERSON, NEW STATESMAN

'Forty years of twentieth-century German history observed through a massive fable about men and dogs. Mad, Gothic, repetitive and bitterly funny' MICHAEL RATCLIFE, THE SUNDAY TIMES

Günter Grass
From the Diary of a Snail £4.95

Probably the most autobiographical of his novels, *From the Diary of a Snail* was first published in 1972. It balances the agonizing history of the persecuted Danzig Jews against an account of Grass's political campaigning with Willie Brandt. Underlying all is the snail, the central symbol that is both a model and a parody of social progress, and a mysterious metaphor for political reform.

'Actual-factual elements are fused with imagined, created things, curt yet marvellously explosive observations: the result is a difficult, dynamic book, like no other novel, possibly not a novel at all, certainly an event in the reader's life and possibly in literature's history' THE SUNDAY TIMES

'A pungent stew of a book using every ingredient to hand; nourishing, but full of strange grisly lumps and bitter flavours' THE GUARDIAN

'Grass is one of the master fabulists of our age and perhaps its supreme dramatist of metaphor' THE TIMES

'A sophisticated critique of Marx, shrewd, moving and funny' NEW STATESMAN

'Grass is one of the few great writers in Europe today' THE SUNDAY TELEGRAPH

The Flounder £5.95

Heralded by many as Grass's finest work, *The Flounder* was first published in 1977. Through the flounder, taken from the fairy story of *The Fisherman and his Wife*, Grass analyses the battle of the sexes with characteristic insight and humour. The nine sections of the book, each representing one month, combine and reinforce a complete reworking of social, political and gastronomic history that seriously questions the roles the male and female may play in mankind's future.

'A masterpiece by one of the most gifted and original of contemporary writers. It is a book that will repay study and rereading. Only a churlish and insular reader could fail to respond to its bold and exhilarating historical sweep, its imaginative recovery of the past, its poetic celebration of food and the arts of cooking' NEW STATESMAN

'None of Grass's novels invite encapsulation. This least of all. The epic range, the communicated excitement, the register of emotions held together by a beautifully reticent structure still allow cameos: even the oblique, understated and heart-stabbing eulogy of Grass's friend Willie Brandt. In small as in large things this is an unforgettable novel' NEW SOCIETY

Michael Ondaatje
In the Skin of a Lion £4.50

'*In the Skin of a Lion* is a poem to workers and lovers. Their labours change them; their skin comes off, and they put on new skin, becoming someone else. "I used to be a searcher. I can work dynamite." As they love, and lose their loves, and love again, their lives (and the shape of the novel) explode into fantastic directions. And yet Michael Ondaatje keeps a promise that he makes in the middle of the novel, "The first sentence of every novel should be: 'Trust me, this will take some time but there is order here, very faint, very human.'" The exquisite, violent scenes of disguise, recognition, new guises are the miraculous events that form the lives of heroes and heroines whom we feel for and think about long after we finish reading'
MAXINE HONG KINGSTON

'A dazzling novel of power and style, dealing with human situations through verbal cinema . . . An extraordinary performance on the level – and beyond – of Ondaatje's *The Collected Works of Billy the Kid* and *Coming Through Slaughter*. He has invented a new form' LEON EDEL

'A magical book. Michael Ondaatje defies the normal distinction between poet and novelist. His writing is consistently tuned to a visionary pitch'
GRAHAM SWIFT

'He's a beautiful writer . . . what he writes about most beautifully is *work*. This is, of course, a rarity in fiction at any time'
NEW YORK TIMES BOOK REVIEW

'Ondaatje mixes fact and fiction, joins documentation and imagination, and emerges with a dauntingly impressive novel . . . rich and generous in its range and subtlety, allusive and highly literate' KEN ADACHI, TORONTO STAR

Mario Vargas Llosa
The Green House £3.95

The Green House was put up across the river from the city of Puira at the edge of the desert. The townspeople laughed at the odd-looking green structure and the stranger who had come into the town to build it. But when the Green House was finished and its first tenants had arrived, the citizens of Puira stopped laughing. For young girls looking for an easier life and the men of Puira, drowning in the monotony and misery of their day-to-day existence, the Green House became a night-time pleasure oasis in the desert. For the religious and moral forces and the indignant matrons of Puira, the Green House became the very incarnation of the Devil – an evil that had to be destroyed at any cost.

'This ample novel succeeds in bringing to life a whole strange, seething society, Peru in the wake of the rubber boom. These figures stand as symbols of their time and place, but first and last they are people, and the achievement of Senor Llosa's fine novel is that proper to the novel: he has made a world, and enhances that of the reader' FINANCIAL TIMES

The Time of the Hero £4.95

The Time of the Hero has been acclaimed by critics around the world as one of the outstanding Spanish-language novels of recent decades. In the author's native Peru, this powerful social satire so outraged the authorities that a thousand copies were publicly burned. The novel is set in the Leoncio Prado Military Academy in Lima. In this microcosm, this city within a city, a group of cadets form another circle in their attempt to break out of the vicious round of sadistic ragging, military discipline, confinement and boredom. But what began as pranks in their first year turns into tragedy by the time the boys reach the third year. The officers' discovery of the theft of a crucial exam sets off a cycle of betrayal, murder and revenge which jeopardizes the entire military hierarchy.

'A number of masterly portraits of cadets entrapped in a snake-pit of adolescent erethism, sadism and ennui . . . a work of undeniable power and skill' SUNDAY TELEGRAPH

Chinua Achebe
The African Trilogy £6.95

Things Fall Apart, Chinua Achebe's first novel, has received widespread critical acclaim since its first publication thirty years ago. It has sold over three million copies and has been translated into more than forty languages. *No Longer At Ease*, its sequel, won the Nigerian National trophy, while *Arrow of God* confirmed Achebe's standing as the founder of modern African fiction. These three novels, collected here in a single volume with a new introduction by the author, chronicle the story of twentieth century West Africa.

'No more important novel than *Things Fall Apart* has been published this century though I think Achebe himself surpassed it in *Arrow of God* . . . six years later' ANGUS CALDER, THE SCOTSMAN

Anthills of the Savannah £3.95

It is the troubled present in West Africa. Two years after the military coup that swept a brilliant young Sandhurst-trained army officer to power there is an uneasy calm in the state of Kangan. His Excellency, defeated in a vital referendum, nervous and embittered, finds comfort in the role of dictator. For those who helped him to power, his oldest friends, the future looks dangerous and uncertain. Chris Oriko, Minister of Information, and Ikem Osodi, poet and editor – innocent when the blood-letting begins – are forced to become players in a drama of love and friendship, betrayal and death, that mirrors the history of their troubled country.

'Achebe's four previous novels earned him the title of Africa's greatest novelist, and nothing has happened since to detract from that . . . This book brings humanity to a world in which we feared it did not exist' RICHARD DOWDEN, THE INDEPENDENT